Environmental Affectivity

Also Available from Bloomsbury

Environmental Ethics, Marion Hourdequin
Why Climate Breakdown Matters, Rupert Read
The Ethics of Giacomo Leopardi, Alice Gibson

Environmental Affectivity

Aesthetics of inhabiting

Omar Felipe Giraldo and
Ingrid Fernanda Toro

BLOOMSBURY ACADEMIC
LONDON • NEW YORK • OXFORD • NEW DELHI • SYDNEY

BLOOMSBURY ACADEMIC
Bloomsbury Publishing Plc, 50 Bedford Square, London, WC1B 3DP, UK
Bloomsbury Publishing Inc, 1359 Broadway, 12th Floor, New York, NY 10018, USA
Bloomsbury Publishing Ireland, 29 Earlsfort Terrace, Dublin 2, D02 AY28, Ireland

BLOOMSBURY, BLOOMSBURY ACADEMIC and the Diana logo
are trademarks of Bloomsbury Publishing Plc

First published in Great Britain 2024
This paperback edition published 2025

Copyright © Omar Felipe Giraldo and Ingrid Fernanda Toro, 2024

Omar Felipe Giraldo and Ingrid Fernanda Toro have asserted their right under the Copyright, Designs and Patents Act, 1988, to be identified as Authors of this work.

Original title: Afectividad ambiental. Sensibilidad, empatía, estéticas del habitar, first edition El Colegio de la Frontera Sur/Universidad Veracruzana, 2020.

Series design by Charlotte Daniels
Cover image: Rainbow Lorikeets Perched In The Garden
(© Svetlana Foote / Alamy Stock Photo)

All rights reserved. No part of this publication may be: i) reproduced or transmitted in any form, electronic or mechanical, including photocopying, recording or by means of any information storage or retrieval system without prior permission in writing from the publishers; or ii) used or reproduced in any way for the training, development or operation of artificial intelligence (AI) technologies, including generative AI technologies. The rights holders expressly reserve this publication from the text and data mining exception as per Article 4(3) of the Digital Single Market Directive (EU) 2019/790.

Bloomsbury Publishing Inc does not have any control over, or responsibility for, any third-party websites referred to or in this book. All internet addresses given in this book were correct at the time of going to press. The author and publisher regret any inconvenience caused if addresses have changed or sites have ceased to exist, but can accept no responsibility for any such changes.

A catalogue record for this book is available from the British Library.

A catalog record for this book is available from the Library of Congress.

ISBN: HB: 978-1-3503-4510-2
PB: 978-1-3503-4514-0
ePDF: 978-1-3503-4511-9
eBook: 978-1-3503-4512-6

Typeset by Integra Software Services Pvt. Ltd.

For product safety related questions contact productsafety@bloomsbury.com.

To find out more about our authors and books visit www.bloomsbury.com
and sign up for our newsletters.

Contents

Preface		vii
1	Environmental Epistemo-Aesthesis: Bodies among Bodies	1
	Beyond Dualisms and Monisms	2
	Multiplicities, Entanglements, Lines, and Trails	11
	Encounters between Bodies	13
	Skins among Skins	20
	Worlds among Worlds	23
	Human Alterity in the Web of Life	25
	Environmental *Ethos*	28
2	Beings Corporealizing Next to Others: Environmental Empathy	35
	Enactive Approach to Neurocognition	37
	Empathy and Affective Connection between Bodies	43
	The Earth Empathizing with Us	57
3	Affective Environmental Knowledge: The Ethics of Contact	63
	Knowing by Living, Knowing by Being	65
	Protection and Maintenance of Vernacular Knowledge	66
	Creativity Specific to a Place	72
	Aesthetics of Vernacular Knowledge	74
	Proportional Lives and Sense of Proportion	80
	The Ethics of Inhabiting-Knowing	83
	Collapse and Environmental Affectivity	89

4	Regime of Affectivity: The Order of Disaffection	93
	Ecology of the Ominous	95
	Violence against the Earth, Violence among Humans	102
	Words, Sensitivity, and Place	108
	The Ecocidal Shadow	113
5	The Desire for Life: The Aesthetic Reorganization of Affections	119
	Counter-Hegemonies of Desire	122
	Aesthetics of Environmental Affectivity	129

Notes	138
Bibliography	144
Index	154

Preface

The only effective answer to the environmental catastrophe of our time is a revolution that not only insists on the radical transformation of the material, political-economic, and technological relations of society, but also addresses in utmost seriousness the affective, sensitive, and sentient dimensions of our being in the world. Any revolution that wishes to reach into the core of our planetary destruction should first and foremost be an ethical-political and aesthetical-poetic revolution that reinstates the body's power and foregrounds sensitivity, feelings, emotions, aesthetics, and empathy. Without the affective dimension, we will not understand these gravely dangerous times or the deep crises of meaning in our contemporary inhabiting. Nor will we be able to grasp the power strategies that loom over human bodies in this collapsing civilization, nor the affective doors that we must open to learn to lovingly inhabit the world.

It is essential to address this topic in environmental thought. To this end we must abandon certain suppositions. We start from the fact that our participation in the world is constitutively affective and sentient, an idea with relative consensus in some branches of psychology, neuroscience, and philosophical phenomenology that attempts to dispute the long-held Enlightenment belief that we are merely "rational beings." We can attribute this belief to the Cartesian tradition, in which "reason" is separate from "affection," and the former is in a position of superiority over the latter. According to this tradition, which today we may call rationalist, mechanistic, objectivist, or positivist, the body's sensory experiences like colors, scents, tastes, and textures are subjective notions or plain obstacles to objective truth and knowledge. The rational, measurable, exact, and precise calculations of Cartesian science made it necessary to dominate and conceal the passions, and to exercise control over the senses, emotions, and affections. This split constituent of modernity made us believe that the two poles, reason and affections, are two impermeable, unrelated, and independent paths, that rationality is the only right way to access knowledge, and that affections are a matter of private life and the universe of artistic creation.

The dominant rationalist paradigm never acknowledged that affection permeates every form of rationality, that being rational is also a matter of affection, and that there is no thought or knowledge free from sensitivity and affection. This idea is central to this book's thesis, since ecocide, the devastation of land, the erosion of life, the implementation of death projects, and the pillaging of the natural fabric are not irrational actions, but instead actions were reason and affection are intertwined. Although the empire of reason in the service of the scientific-technical exploitation of the world is often judged to be the basis of our contemporary civilizational collapse, it should be noted that this instrumental reason is inevitably linked with an affective logic. Rational processes that objectify and exploit the natural fabric cannot occur without an array of affections, sensations, senses, and feelings. Simply put, reason is unviable outside a logic of affective experience. Hence, the civilizational collapse of our time is fundamentally an affective problem, and the environmental crisis is sustained by a very particular form of thought amalgamated with an order of the sensitive experience.

Therefore, rather than "rational beings," as the positivist tradition has made us believe, we are, in the words of Emma León (2011), "affection incarnate," an embodied materiality that does not allow for divisions between mind and body, head and heart, and reason and feeling. Far from the Platonic and Cartesian split on which modern episteme relies, affective incarnation is continuity, mixture, intertwining, and implication; it is the place where rationality is conjugated with the affections of the body, consciousness and unconsciousness, appreciations, sensations, perceptions, appetites, cognitive estimations, moods, valuations, emotions, temperaments, and feelings (León, 2017).

When Pascal said, "the heart has its reasons which reason knows nothing of," he was in a way suggesting that the affective constellation operates under a logic and an order that is difficult to discern (Scheler, 2003). Of course, thought and reason try to express with words the vast sentimental complexity in which conscious and unconscious affections, sensations, desires, moods, impulses, and perceptions are knotted together (León, 2017); but it is likely that "the reasons of the heart" are far from coinciding with the words with which we justify our actions. Which reasons of the heart explain planetary erosion? How do we understand the affections that promote ecosystem disintegration? We hold that the answers to these questions stem from an affective order enmeshed in cultural warps, linguistic gears, aesthetic constellations, and power relations that offer reasons to the heart that reason does not understand. Extinction, the scalding of vital forces, the destructive relationship, and the removal of the living earth are rational acts guided by a sensitive order worth understanding.

This essay on environmental ethics approaches the environmental problem from the perspective of the affective dimension, sensitivity, feelings, and sensory and aesthetic experience based on what we call *environmental affectivity*. To this end, we use the ethics of Baruch Spinoza, the phenomenological and psychoanalytic tradition, aesthetic studies, and Latin American environmental thought. We want to show that building an ethical solution requires a collective affective transformation, that is, a transformation based on the power of the body and the sensitive understanding of conceiving ourselves as bodies among other bodies. The ethical response to the war we have declared on the world demands that we address our numbness in the face of destruction, the insensitivity of the body in the face of death, and affectlessness in the face of devastation: this is perhaps the greatest power of a system that causes so much pain to so many—a pain that cannot be felt as pain, nor as anger, nor as indignation, because this civilization has made us insensitive, reduced the transmission of empathy, and weakened our power to act in the face of destruction. Cultivating sensitivity in a collective way means taking a different path: that we teach ourselves to be touched by the emotion of other bodies, that we regain confidence in our senses, that we break into language and fill it with earth, that we open our sensitive perception numbed by the artifacts of industrial civilization, and that we awaken our affections through contact with different ways of life.

Our intention is not to review the hugely important contributions to environmental ethics by many thinkers from different parts of the world, among whom stand out figures such as Aldo Leopold, Baird Callicott, Ricardo Rozzi, Holmes Rolston, Anna Peterson, Bryan Norton, Stephen Gardiner, or Leonardo Boff. Nor do we intend to raise axiological, deontological, or teleological debates of formal ethics. Rather, this is an attempt to think from other perspectives, other references, and other places of enunciation in which affectivity is the framework of reference for thinking sensitively and aesthetically about the cemetery of bodies and souls begat by our unbridled civilization. Although it should be recognized that in the English-language literature there are recent works that make dialogue between affectivity and environmental philosophy whose contributions are notable (see the books by Oele, 2020; Weik von Mossner, 2017; and de la Bellacasa, 2017), this work is positioned specifically in the context of Latin American environmental thought.

The book is divided into five chapters. The first one presents a theoretical proposal to think about "the environmental" from what we call epistemo-aesthesis: a form of knowledge stemming from the skin, contact, and the senses, in clear allusion to the Colombian thinker Patricia Noguera. We begin with a brief account of a classic discussion of environmental epistemology on ontological monisms and dualisms, to then give rise to our epistemic-aesthetic proposal. Specifically, we question some theoretical approaches that correctly challenge Cartesian dichotomies, but which, in our opinion, continue to examine the environmental problem from two angles: culture versus nature, the human versus the non-human. We believe that it is possible to take a middle path that abandons all Cartesian and Platonic duality, avoids erasing differences, and is clear about the specificities of the human symbolic order—as these environmental epistemes do—but that also understands us as multiplicities, bodies among bodies, worlds among worlds, and skins among skins, all meeting in a semiotic and linguistic network much wider than the human one. Our proposal, following Spinoza's lead, consists in imagining an embodied environmental ethics based on the relations between sentient beings and sustained by affections, sensibility, the senses, and contact. We are interested in understanding ethics as the power that emerges when we know we are affected by encountering the world's sentient beings. We believe that this epistemic way of dealing with "the environmental" helps us imagine an ethics that is discovered by exploring affectivity and awakening the sensitive experience.

In the second chapter we continue our proposal, relying on phenomenological analyses of the cognitive and mental capacities of human beings to investigate how our affections, emotions, minds, and sensory and motor systems are intimately involved with the sensitivities and emotional states of the spaces we inhabit. Specifically, we address empathy understood as the condition necessary for experiencing one's own corporeality enveloped in its affective states by the sensitive state of the inhabited space. We maintain that what the body can do depends on the capacities of the sensitive experience, sensory-motor skills, and the concrete characteristics of the inhabited space.

The idea of *environmental empathy* helps us to say that empathic affection is the glue, the substance, and the myelin that connects the different types of bodies as we interact with them. Thanks to this biological capacity, we can tune in and attune ourselves to the emotionality of a living world, feeling its emotion in our own body, once we learn to care for an Earth that we are part of. For us, environmental empathy is an inter-empathy of many beings touching each other in their life trajectories, in an ecology of inter-sensitivities. Therefore, to inhabit is not to dwell in passive spaces, but to welcome into our sensitive experience the multiple affections, sensitivities, and feelings of an expressive space that listens to us and speaks to us. We are beings in a permanent state of embodiment, protected by a language of the earth composed of sensibilities, aesthetics, empathies, and intuitions.

The third chapter continues this discussion, grounding it in the phenomenology of the environmental knowledge of peasants, fishermen, pastoralists, and indigenous people around the world. We believe that exploring vernacular knowledge offers a pragmatic perspective for understanding how people in their daily life—through direct contact with the beings of the world and their bodily involvement—have understood what kind of mixtures, relationships, aesthetics, and compositions are required for the reproduction of life, and which may lead to the disharmonization of a territory's relationships. In particular, we focus on the aesthetic and perceptual criteria that underlie this type of knowledge.

We hold that one of the main features of environmental knowledge is the acute tuning of the senses to the proportions, balances, and other configurations of what is suitable, as well as to the certainty of everything that is disproportionate and not appropriate for the space. This environmental empathy has been cultivated through the direct relationship with the space, by which people learned the art of tuning into the affective states and aesthetic compositions of the world they inhabit. The exciting thing about recovering vernacular knowledge is that it helps nurture a different kind of environmental ethics because of its capacity to teach the criteria of moderation and sufficiency, the right balance between one's own actions and the actions of other bodies, and the aesthetic confidence that something is going well when it *looks good, sounds good, smells good,* or *tastes good.*

In the fourth chapter we argue that an environmental ethics must also make use of the dark side. We are emotional beings who become enraged, and who cause pain and cruelty. Affectivity is not only love, tenderness, or joy; it is also hatred, envy, pride, and ego. To think that an environmental ethics will lead us immediately and forever to an adequate behavior is a dangerous chimera. Our proposal does not seek human perfectibility. Instead we advance a contextual ethics based on environmental knowledge, which recognizes us as beings who are the depositaries of a collective shadow, of a death drive, so that with both forces we can reach a type of agreement that makes it possible to sustain us in a desire for life.

To address this dark dimension that we host, we have coined the concept of the *regime of affectivity*. Our goal is to name the system of power that creates a reference scheme that orients us as to what to react to sensitively and what to be indifferent to, which elements we are allowed to love and which we must remain numb to. We examine some of the strategies that shape the "ecologies of cruelty": that ominous web through which the sufferings we cause to human beings and to other living beings are intimately intertwined. Through several examples, we show how the *regime of affectivity* weaves sensitive equivalences for committing cruel acts, which are especially clear in the close association between violence against animals and war. We also consider the importance of studying the modern discursive order and its capacity to modify sensibility. We assert that the verbal conventions provided by science and economics affect people's common ways of speaking, guiding affectivity in the anthropocentric terms that suit the predatory enterprise so well. We believe that, according to the project of modern devastation, the best way to reorient collective sensibilities is to strip human discourse of the *language of the earth*, and to expropriate its environmental knowledge, its aesthetic bias and the attunement with the senses of the space, so that destructive energies guide affectivity until we become incapable of empathy.

The book ends by addressing the type of political response that, in our opinion, is indispensable for deconstructing the *regime of affectivity*, denormalizing the ecology of desire and dismantling the anthropocentric discourses that turn the world into a collection of inert objects devoid of a soul. We believe that there is no way to dispute the hegemony of capitalism unless we dismantle this *regime of affectivity* and territorialize an *environmental affectivity*. We can hardly achieve this unless we first understand the sophisticated way in which capitalism creates meaning and mobilizes desire, as explained by psychoanalytic theory. Our working hypothesis here is that to undertake this enterprise, we will have to enter into direct competition for desire with capitalism, creating other imaginary identifications capable of constantly reproducing life as drive. We must take advantage of the fact that one of the major contradictions of the ecologies of cruelty and death is that they activate the drive for life, as evidenced in various peoples' struggles for the defense of life and their bets on different forms of living.

These antagonisms against the death drives that erupt as a sort of rebellious fissure within the system, and that affirm the desire for life, have a fundamental characteristic: they require aesthetics as an essential condition to weave their environmental ethics. This is the resource at hand that, as the environmental knowledge of the peoples teaches, helps to know what is "right" for the space because the senses indicate it so. The aesthetic dimensions inform the ethical actions to be followed; they tune the sensitive experience, the affections, and the thoughts to know what suits the space best, and to tune into the tastes of the sensitive beings of the world.

It is important to clarify that the intention of this text is to outline some ideas and bridges between aesthetics, political ecology, and environmental ethics. Far from closing or exhausting the topics, the objective is to open discussions, to deploy some possible dialogues, and to enunciate some elements of analysis to deepen an eventual research program. The concepts proposed throughout the book are only a provocation, an invitation to explore some intersections between different traditions of thought that have only been partially addressed so far. Several aspects of this work remain to be elaborated with more detail, depth, and rigor in subsequent works. We leave them as open elements with the potential to be addressed by a field of studies on what we call *environmental affectivity*.

***

We would like to use this preface to thank Pierre Madelin, Nicolás Jiménez, and Jorge Wilson Gómez, who were kind enough to read the manuscript and make corrections, critiques, and thoughtful suggestions that helped us improve it considerably. Of course, the omissions, flaws, and problems that persist are entirely our responsibility.

We would also like to briefly describe the spaces that made the emergence of this research possible. The first of these is the beautiful National University of Colombia at Manizales's group on Environmental Thinking, in which the main co-author of this book has participated since 2012. Since that year we have collaborated in different ways, carrying out exchanges, supporting dissertations and academic stays, giving lectures, and creating written displays in accordance with the key ideas advanced by Ana Patricia Noguera. This essay is one more voice that joins the polyphony of a vibrant collective of colleagues and friends.

On the other hand, there were three decisive graduate seminars formally attended by the co-author at the National Autonomous

University of Mexico between 2014 and 2015 for giving theoretical support to the text: *Art and Culture: The Sensitive Order of Affections*, taught by the phenomenologist Emma León; as well as *Ethics in Lévinas* and *Altruism, Empathy, and Understanding*, both taught by Professor Pedro Enrique García, at said university's School of Philosophy and Letters. Thanks to these seminars, often attended as a pair, we were able to delve into the details of empathy, Spinozian ethics, and, in general, the philosophical mechanisms related to affection, sensibility, and aesthetics. The doors opened by these perspectives were key for our subsequent works, among which stand out a master's thesis in humanities sustained in 2019 by the co-author at the Chiapas University of Sciences and Arts on the affectivity of people who try to escape from the established order and live in alternative ways in the city of San Cristóbal de Las Casas (Toro, 2021), and the book *Political Ecology of Agriculture: Agroecology and Post-Development*, especially the chapter dedicated to the government of affections (Giraldo, 2018). Other theoretical approaches have instead been self-taught, such as the study of the neurobiological sciences of cognition from the phenomenological approach and some aspects of psychoanalysis that have long attracted our attention.

This research is also based on the work developed by the co-author on agroecology, which has allowed for a fruitful dialogue of ideas that can be overwhelming due to their excessively theoretical character, and much more practical elements, which have been learned from agroecological peasant and indigenous communities over the last fifteen years in Colombia and Mexico. This has been the empirical basis for showing how environmental ethics is not a desktop reverie, but a pragmatic action for many people, even with the inherent contradictions of the human experience.

Likewise, the opinions expressed here owe much to our own personal experience as apprentices of ecological practices in the place where we have lived for the last four years. We did not want to make bibliographic research stripped of the sensitive experience, because we are sure that it is only possible to enter the affective world from one's own sensitivity, including one's own participation, opening oneself to one's own intimate experience, and investigating firsthand one's own senses and the power of aesthetics. In that sense, we are convinced that our house, located in a rural environment, with the trees that embrace it, the plants in the garden, the bees, butterflies and hummingbirds that visit it, the small vegetable garden with its vegetables and medicinal plants, the rain collected and cleaned in the wetland next to our bedroom, the compost and its worms, the horses and sheep that graze around us, as well as the oak forest that we usually walk in with our three dogs, have not only given us the greatest lesson in philosophy, but have been the best means to explore the sharpening of our senses, the magic of the encounters between bodies, and the phenomenology of environmental knowledge.

We finished writing this book in April 2020, when more than half of the world's population was confined to their homes because of the COVID-19 pandemic. In these trying days for many people, the planet experienced a respite from our indolent actions. Factories came to a standstill, cars stayed in their garages, society suspended its frenetic consumerist obsessions, inhabitants of megacities once again saw the blue horizon previously covered by the gray smog of fuel pollution, global warming slowed down, rivers regained their crystalline appearance, and, as in fairy tales, deer, foxes, wild boars, monkeys, pumas, ducks, swans, and other animals forsaken by our toxic habits suddenly began to be seen roaming the cities, recovering spaces that until just a few days before appeared so threatening and so petty to them. In those magical days, thanks to our absence, the force of life suddenly recovered its cycles and its rhythms, making us remember, with its affective gestures, that our delusions of domination, our self-worship by the noisy artifacts we design and by the frenetic drive to rarefy life, is nothing more than a mirage capable of hiding our insignificance, our smallness in the thin film of the Earth's atmosphere. On the scale not of months or years, but of just a few days, the breath of life returned so placidly with its aesthetic orders and sensibilities to remind us of our limits, the forces that surpass us, the fragility of our place in the cosmos, to tell us, in its own language, that we need only decide one day to abandon this way of living and radically rethink how we inhabit the world.

1

Environmental Epistemo-Aesthesis: Bodies among Bodies

In this first chapter we will use environmental epistemology to approximate an ethics that allows us to be moved with awe and respect for life, to awaken potency before what is sensed, and to inhabit poetically as we recognize ourselves as wandering bodies that encounter other bodies. To this end, we begin by considering the modern episteme and other proposals associated with environmental thought through a discussion of ontological dualisms and monisms. In particular, we wonder if it is possible to open a middle path that abandons all duality but does not erase differences. By asking this question we critically examine the concept of "episteme-ology" and its association with a rationalized "logos" that lacks affection and sensibility; and the "environmental," understood in relation to the surroundings and in opposition to the human and the social, to offer a proposal based on *multiplicities*, bodies among bodies, and encounters between radical alterities.

The question we are asking—in line with philosopher Patricia Noguera's proposal—is whether it is possible to go further than epistemology and unlock an epistemo-aesthesis that places sensations, sensibility, the senses, and affections in the foreground. We also ask if we can imagine an environmental ethics that starts from the skin and from contact, an *ethos* that is undertaken from our own sensitive body, understood as the territory from which the universe is sensed and inhabited. Our intention is to contribute to the aestheticization of environmental though by recognizing that the encounter in what we call "environment" is not between subjects, and surely not between subjects and objects, but between skins, between diverse membranes that touch each other in an affective entanglement of bodies composed of multiple mixtures that experience their universe, thanks to their embodied affectivity. We want to continue a path paved by many environmental thinkers on whose shoulders we stand to imagine how we can promote loving contact between the world's sentient beings and therefore contribute to an aestheticization of inhabiting.

Beyond Dualisms and Monisms

Environmental epistemology has insisted that the environmental crisis is an ontological crisis, a consequence of how we understand our being and our relationship with other beings. In general, in this understanding we place ourselves on the highest level of the manifestations of being, imagining the rest of the entities as inert objects, resources available at our complete disposal. In philosophy, this separation of human beings from other beings has been attributed to the metaphysical thinking that dates to Plato and which consolidated in modernity with Cartesian positivism. This tradition has separated subject from object, based on the notion that the world "is" somehow an objective world, and it follows that knowledge is about the subject forming an idea that is faithful to the object. In fact, it is possible to reach "the truth" the more accurately one represents the object one wishes to know. In positivist epistemology, the existence of things is independent of the subject, and, consequently, it is possible to know the world "as is." In fact, the greater the distance between the knowing subject and the known object, the greater the objectivity.

Environmental thought asserts that with this split constituent to modern thinking, on the one hand, human beings came to represent themselves as the center of the world, as possessors of everything that exists around them; and on the other hand, they ended up conceiving of what they call "nature" as an inert object, an available resource, a thing ready to be manipulated by science and technology (Heidegger, 1996). Environmental thought also asserts that modern ontology is not only characterized by the subject/object split but is a specific type of ontology characterized by other polar dyads such as mind/body, culture/nature, reason/affections, civilized/primitive, masculine/feminine, secular/sacred, individual/community, and human/animal (Plumwood, 2002, 2005). The problem, as Arturo Escobar (2013) has said, is not so much that dualisms exist, since many other traditions such as Taoism, Buddhism, and a large part of the indigenous peoples in different continents have based their ontologies on interconnected dualities under the principle of complementarity. The problem is that in modernity the first part of the dualism—the subject, the mind, the culture, the reason, the civilized, the masculine, and the secular—is separated and placed in a position of superiority over the subordinate element of the binarism—the body, the nature, the affections, the primitive, the feminine, and the sacred.[1]

It is therefore well recognized in critical thinking that the environmental crisis is not a geological or ecological problem, but a civilizational mess produced by a particular type of ontology and generated by ontological thought and its constitutive splits (Leff, 2018). This crisis or collapse is the consequence of an ontology based on the modern "I" and the belief that the world is composed of many "Is" separate from each other—humanity as the sum of its individuals—and separate from the other beings in the world—the rest: nature. From this fragmented self-determination emerges an ethics of knowledge based on uncovering the truth through science and then intervening and manipulating what is known with the help of technology, overcoming scarcity, and providing what the economy has dictated as necessary for only one of Earth's sentient beings.

From this diagnosis of the environmental crisis arises a choir of voices of thought that mean to overcome the dualistic ontology and to shift toward other ontologies connected to the webs of life. This is the basis that brings together most environmental thinkers who, in different parts of the world, denounce the split and offer ontological, epistemic, and *relational* ethical solutions to the devastation that arises as a symptom of conceiving of our being as separate from nature.

One of the best known of these voices is Arne Naess (2007) and his environmental ethics called *deep ecology*, whose bet is to perform a surgical suture, to erase the disjunction, and to provide a solution in terms of the identification of the "I" with nature. For supporters of this environmental ethics, it is necessary to overcome the separation between human beings and nature—given that there can be no ontological division between two realms: human and non-human—and there is an urgency to understand the universe as an interconnected, seamless whole. Deep ecologists argue that we must abandon the split, that we must replace the schism by a holistic understanding, that everything is interrelated and interdependent on everything else, and that we must enter a process of unification, understanding that everything that exists is actually "part of" and indistinguishable from everything else (Fox, 1984). They claim that the self-concept as interrelational beings and the identification of the "I" with the totality is the basis for the impulse to care, not due to altruism or a moral "ought," but because caring for the other is part of the interest of existence itself.

If we wanted to conduct an archaeological investigation of holism in Western philosophy, we would have to go back to Baruch Spinoza,[2] who proposed a path opposed to Cartesian dualism. Spinoza (2011) challenged the view that we could separate human beings from the realm of nature, as if they were "an empire within an empire" rather than nature itself. On the contrary, for him there is only a single, absolutely infinite substance. What we call creatures are not so;

they are merely modes or forms of existence of that substance. All existents are not beings but entities, ways of being of that substance (Deleuze, 1980). Undoubtedly, this vision can be compared to other traditions such as Lao Tzu's Taoism or some ontologies of the ancestral peoples of Abya Yala.[3] Whatever the path, these sources have inspired some environmental thinkers who have sought to overcome Cartesian dualism through a holistic view of the world. Among them are not only the proponents of deep ecology, but other authors, among which it is worth highlighting the complex thought of Edgar Morin (1986), the web of life of Fritjof Capra (1998), the Gaia hypothesis of James Lovelock (2007), the post-structuralism of Gilles Deleuze and Félix Guattari (2004), and the environmental anthropology of Descola and Pálsson (2001) or Viveiros de Castro (1998).

This type of stance that seeks reunification in an organic whole has been questioned by some thinkers who have offered good arguments about the dangers of solving *ontological dualism*—the separation of human beings and nature—through *ontological monism*, that is, through their unification. Among the sharpest critics is ecofeminist Val Plumwood (2002), who agrees with deep ecologists in that it is necessary to overcome dualisms; indeed much of her work deals with them systematically. However, she asserts, it is neither necessary nor desirable to try to assimilate the other, erasing their distinctiveness and difference. According to the Australian philosopher, to overcome dualism it is necessary to maintain a balance between continuity and difference, since the dialectic between connection and otherness is the key to non-instrumental interaction. Plumwood argues that the loss of tension between the different and the alike has been one of the main characteristics of the history of colonization. The process has always been the same: devouring the other, denying its difference, and incorporating it into a totalizing process.

Plumwood (2002) says that there is an acrimonious arrogance when boundaries are not observed and differences are not recognized; these are ultimately the basis of respect. Of course we must recognize human continuity with the natural world, she argues, but we must also recognize nature's distinctiveness, even its independence from us, and the distinction of its needs from our own. For Plumwood, it is not useful or even necessary to fuse humans and nature to overcome dichotomies, since the ethics of care promoted by ecofeminism also requires distance and the recognition of difference, so that the other is not seen as a projection of the self. She proposes moving toward a type of ethic that allows for both continuity and difference, and avoids abstraction, dissolution, and blurring the distinction between human beings and nature.

Mexican environmental philosopher Enrique Leff (2004, ch. 2) has also criticized *ontological monism*, although he has done it in dialogue with green anarchist Murray Bookchin (1990), who, from a different standpoint, has proposed combining the ecological and sociocultural orders. For Leff, it is impossible to aspire to a unifying totality that fuses the materiality of the world and the symbolic in a sameness. We cannot ignore that the symbolic order, through meanings, language, and the organization of culture, weaves the life of human beings, both in their social relations and in their power relations, and that they can in no way be subsumed within a unifying order. Leff draws on Lacan to say that there is nothing less natural than the subject and consciousness, desire, and the symbolic order. For this reason, it is useless to try to fuse and confuse the two orders; it is impossible to dissolve the separation between the Real and the Symbolic and to aspire to a totalizing and all-encompassing vision of the world.

Let us recall that Lacanian psychoanalysis—on which part of Leff's work is based—holds that humans have nothing to do with the natural order, obeying rules alien to nature. Johnston (2010) has gone so far as to say that we inhabit the plane of *antiphysis*, a place we call "culture" (Ruiz, 2018). The subject must make do from this subjective foundation, that is, from the "non-natural" symbolic universe, to encounter the Real of the *physis*. For this the subject constructs signifiers in language whose function is to mediate between him and the Real. The subject has no choice but to make signifiers in order to create meaning in life, for that is where he finds his den. When we say the word "Nature" or "Mother Earth," we are not referring to the Real world itself. It is instead a designation,[4] a signifier that serves to produce some historicity in human beings. For Lacan there is an insurmountable split, and therefore we need the symbolic structure to relate to the world (Ruiz, 2018).

Leff uses this psychoanalytic explanation that vindicates the inevitable split of the subject from nature to question the proposals that mean to solve the divorce between society and nature by greening the social order. Leff agrees with Plumwood that an ontology of difference and an ethics of otherness are necessary, rejecting of course the Cartesian split but accepting that there is a dialectic: a play of relations between culture and nature; an ontological hybridization between different differentiated orders, the first explained from a symbolic perspective, and the second with thermodynamics as a necessary condition for the reproduction of life on Earth. Leff's proposal (2014, p. 254) is then not to make "a monistic imposition of the ontological difference," but to refocus thought toward the immanence of life, toward the ecological conditions of the planet, so that "a new coherence between the Real and the Symbolic" can be founded.

Although both authors start from the metaphysical fragmentation of Western culture as the origin of the environmental crisis, they agree in saying that the path of *ontological monism* is not free of problems. They present good arguments against annulling the difference of otherness and the symbolic order inherent to the human animal.

Colombian environmental philosopher Augusto Ángel Maya (1996), who nestles in Darwinian and Spinozian thoughts, proposes something in between. Like Lacan, Plumwood, and Leff, he argues that both the ecosystem and culture have their own order. According to Ángel Maya, the human species evolved along a different path than plants and animals, and that path led the species to be banished forever from the ecosystemic paradise and to become a symbolic creature. However, Ángel Maya surreptitiously proposes a dialogue between Spinoza and Darwin when he affirms that culture, as an adaptive form, is part of nature. Although we no longer belong to the ecosystemic order, nor follow its laws, nor belong to any ecological niche, we are still part of nature: the emergence of a single immanent substance from which it is impossible to separate ourselves. Culture is an extension of evolution, he assures, "a fact as natural as biological evolution." Ángel Maya is categorical in affirming that "it is nature that becomes culture. Culture does not constitute a foreign intrusion in nature's order. It is a phase of nature itself" (1996, p. 58). With this explanation Ángel Maya evades the Lacanian discussion on whether culture is part of nature, and at the same time he maintains the distinction between each order.

Thus we have Plumwood, Leff, and Ángel Maya defending the idea of the dialectic between both orders: culture and ecosystems, the symbolic and the Real. However, the Latin American philosophers differ on whether culture is part of the natural domain. Rather than settle this debate—which would differ from an evolutionary or post-structuralist perspective, or from linguistics or Lacanian psychoanalysis—both positions, although contradictory, provide very important elements for the creation of an environmental epistemo-aesthesis. It is not our intention to make a conciliatory synthesis between the two, which is neither possible nor desirable. Instead we think it is necessary to take seriously Leff and Ángel Maya's argument according to which environmental thought should focus on the symbolic sphere—in language and its processes of signification—and from there create other processes of symbolization to achieve an *ontology of difference* and an ethics of otherness. On the other hand, we consider it necessary to do so from the field of interrelation, interdependence, and continuity among all the manifestations and expressions of the universe.

To do this fundamental work, we think it is not enough to approach the problem from the two orders of culture and nature. Although we must always consider human characteristics, their symbolic frameworks, language, and their signification processes—as Lacan or Leff have insisted—maintaining ontological dualism will not do, whether in dialectical terms or in terms of correspondence, complementarity, reciprocity, and non-hierarchy, to the extent that we continue to think of the epistemic problem of the environmental crisis from two domains: the human and the non-human.

What we mean is that we should not keep trying to solve the metaphysical divisions between people and the rest of the beings with the same category of pairs for the relationship. In other words, the suggestion is not to pose the problem as a matter of articulation between the human being as a category on the one hand, and everything else—whether it is called ecosystem, nature, or the Real *physis*—as another category on the other hand. The "nature" signifier—so persistent in our culture but so foreign to most non-Western cultures—is too broad, all-encompassing, and abstract to include everything that does not fit within the human order. We are likely to remain prisoners of Cartesian thinking when we divide the world into dyads, pairs, or binomials in which "the human" or "culture" is always one part, and we leave the rest as another pole. Although Augusto Ángel Maya's intermediate solution is interesting in that it includes culture as an evolutionary emergence from nature, in our opinion we are still plodding in an attempt to deal with the other proposed dyad: ecosystem/culture. Whatever the path, we continue to think about where to place human order in some kind of dualism.

In any case, just as *ontological monism* has its difficulties in denying difference, obviating the symbolic status of "the human" and the thermodynamic conditions of life on Earth, *ontological dualism* based on dialectics and non-hierarchy has the problem of continuing to conceive of "the environmental" from the perspective of two poles. The universe is too big to contain the ontology of the "non-human" as a single and unique order, and we are too minuscule in the cosmic immensity to attempt to encompass a gigantic order called "Culture." We therefore must dissolve the metaphysical dichotomy, but also ontological monism and dialectical duality, and set out on another path, another middle road.

For this we need to say, as Deleuze (1973) does, that Cartesian metaphysical opposition is not actually between the one and the other—the human versus the non-human—but between the one and the multiple, that is, "the opposition between something that can be declared as one, and something that can be declared as multiple" (para. 13). However, here is the rub: the human cannot be categorized as "the one," given the multiplicity of worlds and cosmo-existences (Blaser, 2009) that populate the earth. As environmental anthropology has denounced, there is nothing that we can reduce to "the Human" in singular, as if we could group symbolic diversity into a universalizable category. And since it makes even less sense to conceive of "nature" as a single dimension agglutinated in a single domain, insofar as it is multiple by definition, it is pointless to make any kind of opposition, even dialectical, between the one and the multiple. There is no more human/nature relationship, and we can instead affirm together with the French philosopher: "There is nothing that is One, nothing that is multiple; everything is multiplicities" (para. 27).

Our proposal, following this Deleuzian argumentation, is to completely escape from the pair's nature and culture, or ecosystem and culture, and radically address the phenomenon of *multiplicities*. That is, we will not start with two orders or two dimensions, but instead with the *multiplicity* that makes up life. Moreover, this alternative seeks to reactivate and foreground the subalternities of patriarchal domination, such as the body, affections, sensibilities, and the sacred. The challenge is putting *multiplicities* into play without erasing differences while respecting radical otherness at the same time.

Multiplicities, Entanglements, Lines, and Trails

Multiplicities, as Deleuze and Guattari (2004) have said, are rhizomatic, in the sense that they are ramifications that go in all directions and where any point can be connected to another point. In *multiplicities* there is no subject or object, no dualism. They are instead comprised of branching lines with no beginning or end. Well, to address this concept of *multiplicities* in environmental thought, we consider it worthwhile to study the recent work developed by English anthropologist Tim Ingold (2015). Although he does not reference Deleuze and Guattari, we think that his elaboration on *Lines* gives an excellent initial picture of what we want to say here.

According to Ingold (2012), the environment can be regarded as an entanglement that includes multiple human and non-human components. For him, all creatures that make up this relational entanglement are transient creatures that accompany each other in the world in which they are all present and, through their actions and movement, they create the conditions for others to live. What the anthropologist is trying to convey is that what we call "environment" is a tangle of intertwining paths or threads. Far more than a relationship that emerges from the ecosystem-culture relationship—as Augusto Ángel Maya thinks—the environment is a knot of *multiplicities*, a web of entanglements. Ingold (2012, p. 29) draws on Swedish geographer Torsten Hägerstrand (1976) to say that by imagining each component of the environment, "including humans, plants, animals, and things, all at the same time," on a continuous trajectory of movement, encountering other trajectories, we can see how the various components become interwoven.

Indeed, in illustrating such an environment, Ingold (2015) stresses, we might well begin by drawing a sinuous, colored line on a piece of paper resembling a creature's path. Since this creature is not alone, we would have to draw other lines, each with a different color, representing the paths of other expressions of life that have arrived at the same point by other routes. If we were to add paths to this colorful illustration, little by little the image would become more and more convoluted. The lines would intertwine, forming a tangle, lump, or knot. But the creatures do not stay there. Instead they wander on, walking, following their paths along other routes, and so the knot that we can draw is only provisional. We would then have to imagine that the lines are unraveling to make other knots, to then unravel again and form new knots and so on. This Gordian knot is the "environment," Ingold (2012) asserts: a weave of threads that are the paths of diverse creatures and objects that inhabit the same place. If we were to see it from the inside, says Hägerstrand (1976), we could see how the tips of the pathways sometimes push forward, sometimes backward, going back and forth in all directions, feeling embraced by the tapestry as they move.

Each path left by each creature is a type of lifeline. Among the inhabitants that make up these trails are countless types of beings: some crawling, some walking, some flying, some digging, some swimming, some furrowing with their flagella in the ether, some moving through their rhizomes and roots beneath the earth, some on the time scales of geological formations, all of them together, inhabiting the same place. And in this entanglement there are no borders or exteriors because life cannot be contained, it cannot be enclosed. There is no environment that surrounds us. There are no limits or boundaries, but rather meshes of lines in which "different paths become completely entangled. This snarl, this mesh of crisscrossing lines has no outside and no inside, only openings and pathways" (Ingold, 2015, p. 148).

From this perspective, all the components of this great plot, Ingold (2012) continues, are not beings, but rather becomings: bird becomings, tool becomings, plant becomings, human becomings, bacteria becomings, going back and forth, forming a large pattern of interweaving lines. We are not a split order trying to make connections but beings that have always lived together with others. It is difficult to say where a person ends and their environment begins. We are so entangled in the tapestry of paths that we cannot think of ourselves as being outside, trying to access "nature"—with all that is associated with exteriority—much less think of the non-human as "the environment" or "medium." In the rhizome of life, each line is always moving, intertwining with other lines that are also moving, fraying here and spinning there, weaving together the great web of life.

Encounters between Bodies

This notion of entanglements and enmeshments in constant movement provides a first image—not entirely satisfactory, but introductory—for creating environmental epistemo-aesthesis. On our part, and inspired by Spinoza, the Latin American environmental thought of Colombian Ana Patricia Noguera and Argentine José Luis Grosso, Mexican phenomenologist Emma León, the Chilean neurobiologist Francisco Varela, and the Mexican aesthete Katya Mandoki, we want to follow Ingold's approach but from the notion of *bodies among bodies*.

First we must ask, what traces paths, trails, and routes? What tangles and untangles? These questions lead us immediately to the answer that what moves and wanders, what builds the environment as a zone of entanglement, is the body. We speak of stone-bodies, water-bodies, air-bodies, fire-bodies, plant-bodies, animal-bodies, and human-bodies. To answer this inquiry it is worthwhile to refer to the examination of the human body and the issue of whether the body is our "self," as asked in the Buddhist texts of the Abhidharma.

Following Varela, Thompson, and Rosch's (1997, p. 89) explanation, we treat our body as if it were our "I." The body is the place where the senses are; we perceive the world from the body, "but do we really believe that the body is equal to the self?" Let us consider how our body's configuration is permanently changing. Cells are in a process of constant change—it is estimated that every hour we replace more than one million skin cells—so that an organism is not the same even on the same day and is never identical to itself. With the processes of cellular renewal an individual changes many of its components from one hour to the next, and in that sense, we cannot say that it is the same individual. But in another sense, it is not completely different either since it maintains its structure and organizational pattern.

Let us examine the number of small bodies that our human body harbors. As has been described, it is inhabited by some forty-eight trillion bacteria, sixty trillion viruses, several billion fungi, and millions of other mites, which together are far more numerous than the cells of the body itself. Perhaps we may say, "I have a body that belongs to me," but could we say that those microbe-bodies that live in our bodies belong to us? (Varela, Thompson, and Rosch, 1997). Consider water. We know that our body is 70 percent water, but is that water part of my "I"? Science has told us that every molecule of water has existed for billions of years. Water came to Earth in asteroids and comets, and from there it has been circulating through rocks, animals, and plants. Before that water made up most of my body, it was in oceans, rain, frozen in polar ice caps, and it was part of bacteria and dinosaurs (Jha, 2015). That water will not remain still but will keep on flowing once it leaves the body and wanders on, following its paths of movement.

There is no basis for saying that there is anything in any of the routes[5] that can be called in a delimited way a "body," insofar as we cannot imagine any body separated from its exterior by the boundary of its skin, or its scales, bark, or shell. Where does a body really begin and end? Can a body be thought of as separate from what it inhabits and what inhabits it? Is there such a thing as an I-body? Perhaps we should not define the body by a unitary essence but by the set of relations that make it up, by the dynamics of corporeal and extra-corporeal relations that form it. In fact, perhaps the word "body" is not a noun, but a verb, an act. We are not a body; we are always in the process of becoming embodied, of inter-incarnating ourselves through different encounters (León, 2017). The configuration of that which we wrongly call the "I" is nothing but a series of encounters, of paths, as Ingold would say, of wandering bodies that meet other bodies, but which also break away from each other to follow other paths where they will meet other bodies.

Buddhist philosopher Juan Arnau (2017, p. 111) reminds us how Berkeley "assured that the taste of an apple does not reside in the apple itself, nor in the person who tastes it, but in the encounter between the two." The apple is the result of a flow of encounters, like the seed and the rain, the microorganisms in the soil and the tree, the harvest and the farmer's hand, just as a person is the fruit of the encounter between their parents and their gametes, and of a multitude of encounters in their life story. The long trajectory of the apple, as José Luis Grosso would say,[6] is the one that touches us, the one that comes to our tongue. The pleasure of the apple's taste is the pleasure of the relationship, not of what is inside—taste buds— or outside—the apple's skin and its juice—but the encounter between both surfaces, a relationship between bodies. The apple touches me, I touch it. We are always in contact with the beings of the world, which is why Arnau (2017, p. 112) says that the person and the apple are encounters "in a chain whose origin we cannot locate." We are bodies among bodies, meeting each other. We are energetic, chemical, and sensitive encounters at different scales: from the scale of the apple and the person's mouth, and the subatomic particles that underlie it, to the scale of constellations. And besides being distinct scales, we are encounters between different speeds: from the vertiginous movement of electrons or the accelerated rate of reproduction of bacteria, to the slow movement of a tree through the ground or the glacial speed of stones. We are entanglements between different types of bodies, crisscrossing through dynamic paths in a relationship amid scales and speeds.

Our existence is an inter-existence, an inter-being, flowing, incarnating ourselves, creating states that fade away to give rise to new states. With our acts and the acts of others, with our sensibilities and the sensibilities of others, we are "here," transforming ourselves, exchanging, intertwining among the different expressions of life, interacting within a sentient universe that encompasses us. Spinoza taught that we are expressions of life, "life within life," as Emma León (2017) would say, guarded by the interactions of our relational entanglements. What we are depends on what manages to get entangled, on the compositions of many diverse organisms, each of which is composed of other organisms. Like Russian dolls, our life is only possible thanks to the lives we carry inside us (Haskell, 2012). It is not that we are, but that we inter-are, as the Buddhist master Thich Nhat Hanh (1975) would put it.

"Bodies among bodies" accounts for the inter-incarnation or co-corporealization that arises from the encounter between a multiplicity of forces, energies, sensitivities, moods, and affections that interact dynamically (León, 2017). This view adopts a middle path that takes seriously the interdependencies of Spinozian thought and the critique of the elimination of difference. There is no monism, understood as totalization, but instead encounters between radical alterities. Each body contained in the various corporeal forms, whether flesh and bone, thorns and scales, bark and wood, interacts differently with the bodies it encounters. Radical otherness and the renunciation of any totalizing monism lie in the morphological, historical, phylogenetic specificities, and structural possibilities of each type of body.

Thus we can say that the radical difference begins with the body. For it is not the same to have "hands instead of claws, lungs instead of gills, arms instead of wings, skin instead of scales," as Emma León (2017, p. 56) asserts. Each one experiences the sensible world in their own way and lives their processes of co-corporealization in the being-among-other-bodies, sometimes amalgamating and merging, sometimes separating and following new paths. We are-being thanks to movement, change, impermanence; thanks to the phenomena of interweaving between matter and energy. Bodies, their fluids, their thermal forces, their vital energies are transformed by other fluids, other thermal forces, other vital energies. Life within life lies precisely in the radical otherness that characterizes the encounters between different bodies (León, 2017).

However, it is necessary to point out that the encounters are not random, as Tim Ingold implies with his knot. They obey a self-organizing pattern that explains some of the regularities of our planet, which amalgamate to create the proportions and beauty of the flow of life. Turing's (1990) mathematics have shown how the zebra's stripes, the jaguar's spots, the arrangement of fingers on the hand, the snail's spiral, the arrangement of bird feathers, the spatial location of predators and prey, the brain's convolutions, the ear's hair cells, or the shapes of vegetation all obey a particular interaction of molecules that follow reiterative combinations. In other words, molecules spontaneously self-organize and feedback following a repetitive biological pattern. The lines left by Ingold's trails, rather than entanglements are self-organizing patterns, fractals, and repetitive designs that explain the resemblance between a leopard's skin and certain aquatic formations; between a zebra's spots and the ridges that form on sand dunes; between marine corals and salt marshes; between the eye of a hurricane and a mollusk's shell; or between reptiles' skin and beehives.

The encounters are much more than fortuitous, disorganized encounters. They follow an aesthetic logic. Many processes meet with other processes and, when linked, they compose a dance of groupings and regroupings that follow a necessary succession (Hägerstrand, 1976). It is precisely because the various becomings do not meet in a disorganized way but follow the patterns we identify in the various biological and geological formations that we can perceive as the beauty of our living planet. The environment is therefore a process of encounters, of entanglements—we agree with Ingold—but the process is self-organized and dynamic in long coevolutionary trajectories by which symmetries, proportions, and repetitive forms are formed in unsuspected places. We consider all biological patterns to be beautiful: the symmetry in the butterfly's wings, the balance on animals' faces, the birds' color combinations, and the harmony that shines from the proportions that emerge in the weaves of life.

This way of thinking about the relational mysteries of Mother Earth contrasts with the strange modern notion of "nature," understood as a backdrop or exterior. We are paths, aggregates of movements following patterns in the flow of the elements and their cycles, aggregates of the intertwining of *multiplicities* of becomings. The key is not to start from a detached world and then go meet it, but to understand ourselves from the beginning as "already always inhabiting." When we speak of human beings and nature, it could seem that people are on one side and nature on the other. But the *multiplicity* that we inhabit and that inhabits us is not opposite to people, it is not an external object. Humans are not detached from nature (Heidegger, 1994). We are "just here" (Kusch, 1976) with others, receiving the sensations and potencies of other bodies we meet.

In this decentered magma there is an ontological inconsistency: there is no center to point at and say, "there it is." There seems to be an ontology of the body, but there is also no grounding it in something we can call, in a bounded way, the "Body." It is a sprawling ontology, empty of any center, distributed throughout the territory of bodies "among" other bodies. And when we say "among," we are thinking of the place where the self and the other coexist. It is an invitation to think not only of the body, but also of the bridge, which is, after all, the one that allows the colliding edges to appear (Heidegger, 1994). It is by the bridge, which here we call "among," that the relationship is established between the enveloping boundaries of my own body and the other bodies I depend on to maintain the pattern of organization that constitutes me. It is the boundary of my envelopment that allows me to cross the bridge from side to side, bringing together a structurally coupled embodiment and an inhabited outer space.

Environmental epistemo-aesthesis understands that no body can exist without the others, since each acquires its properties because of its interactions with the others. However, there is also a paradox, because in this ontology there is no fusion or loss of difference, as Plumwood says. Each body, while remaining united with others, distinguishes itself as a differentiated unit. It is a sort of dialectic between continuity and difference in which there is an indissoluble union between diverse modes of life, but it is precisely this vital link of co-determinations that allows each organism to maintain its own individuality (Varela, 2000).

Although in its structure and function the body is connected, spliced, and interrelated to other bodies, it does not escape an envelope that encloses its own organs, organized in a coherent pattern. Although made of extraterrestrial water and stardust, it is organized into a unit that regenerates itself from itself. It is a body that, despite being composed of multiple flows of materials, genes, and energies from diverse sources—which in turn are composed of other sources that are also conditioned by other sources—maintains its unity and difference. Is it a body? Yes, there is a body. But it is a mestizo body, made of mysterious mixtures and compositions, which relates to other bodies also made up of inscrutable mixtures and compositions. It is a body that borrows for very short times the water that flows through the organism, the materials that feed it, the energy that animates it, and all the exterior forces that find in it a momentary place to dwell.

The epistemic problem of what we call "the environmental" consists in understanding that there is no separation, no divorce, but instead dynamic entanglement, a pregnancy of proliferations that follows aesthetic patterns. But at the same time, the issue is understanding that among the *multiple* we are different. This diversity of encounters explains life. We inhabit with other alterities, being inter-penetrated, implicated, and involved in the thick warp of life. That is why we are life within life, a form of life that maintains its own structure and specifications, which does not dissolve into a greater whole but cannot be imagined apart from the others.

Skins among Skins

The magic of encounters happens through touch, perhaps the most ancient and primordial of the senses. As Katya Mandoki (2013) explains, we are membranous beings that maintain our own configuration through tactile contact. Protected by our coatings, we do not dissolve, but thanks to them, we are also exposed to the world and we are touched by others. The different types of skins, whether they are scales, exoskeletons, phyllospheres, or sheaths, isolate as well as connect. We meet each other through cutaneous expression, feeling skin against skin. By touching and being touched, life originated and gradually expanded. The edges of atoms recognized themselves through the edges of other atoms. This way, matter was able to feel other matter, to perceive it through its edges. Recognizing and attracting each other through their sensitivity, the atoms assembled, creating molecules. Shapes detected other shapes, allowing themselves to be seduced and impressed, forming precise connections like the pieces of a jigsaw puzzle.

One by one, *multiplicities* were assembled, made possible by their capacity to feel, to be affected and to affect, and by putting surfaces in contact. Touching, caressing, and groping, they created affectations and new forms. Monomers became polymers; amino and carboxyl groups became amino acids; and amino acids became proteins through peptide bonds. The story of coevolution is the story of interactions, of encounters and links between the skins of molecules that allowed for the emergence of unicellular organisms; it is the story of assemblies between the skins of cells that became indivisible, and with them emerged multicellular organisms. Coevolution, or better yet, the transformation of the webs of life, is a story that can be told from the point of view of feeling, sensation, and sensitivity; of sensitive molecules that reacted to stimuli triggered by encounters with other molecules; of sensitive cells that knew their environment and were affectively coupled, conforming to an autopoietic pattern of organization.

The breath of life is the breath of sensation, touch, and feeling. From a bacterium to a whale, through an ecosystem, up to the vault of constellations, we are all, without exception, sensitive and aesthetic beings who react to encounters with other bodies and transmit sensations to other bodies rhizomatically. Thus, molecular shapes touch the three-dimensional shapes of other molecules, which, at another level, mean that cell walls are entering into a sensitive relationship with cell walls of different types. Different beings, through their skins, come into contact in many ways, even at a distance, as happens when cells touch each other by means of hormones, enzymes, cytokines, or peptides that flow through the organism, or when the cellular couplings that form an individual join with other cellular arrangements of other individuals by means of different chemical mediators.

We inhabit between recurrent intertactualities and our existence even begins with a caress between the skin of an ovum and the skin of a spermatozoon. The odyssey of life can be told through the stories of the sheaths, the coatings, the membranes, and the skins that meet one another. By means of a sensation, of contact, each sensitive body responds affectively to the presence of other bodies, resonating, vibrating, and intoning, but also moving away or fleeing so as not to become prey to them. In our coevolutionary history we have developed different types of sensors to affectively detect and react to stimuli, signs, and impressions from other bodies. It is in the course of an aesthetic history of encounters between sensors and stimuli that the web of life has organized itself rhythmically, unfolding in its wake the fractals of sounds, colors, temperatures, vibrations, flavors, contours, and thicknesses that characterize our majestic blue planet.

Mandoki suggests that beauty is how life self-organizes. It is the miracle in which matter was able to perceive and feel other matter because beauty fulfills a function of attraction for an organism. Life is erotic because, to stimulate an encounter, it must exhibit, impress, and seduce. It must create a message that will be captured by another body, which will adjust its perception to whatever is significant to it. Bodies, whether a molecule, a cell, a microorganism, or a macroorganism, sensitively detect the stimuli produced by other bodies, reacting to them emotionally, either being attracted—to absorb nutrients or reproduce—or repulsed—to avoid toxins or predators. Aesthesis, says Mandoki, is the lamp that illuminates the world through our sensitivity to select and differentiate between that which enables life and that which is contrary to it.

We can say that all creatures, from the humblest molecules to the largest mammal, need to perceive, know, and react affectively to the world in order to coordinate behaviors and to fit between the compositions of life's different modes and expressions, and that it is thanks to the skin that we can come into contact among *multiplicities*.

Worlds among Worlds

Biologist Jakob von Uexküll (1942) introduced the concept of *umwelt* or "surrounding world" to express how humans and other animals perceive the shared world in a differentiated way. The reality perceived by an organism is what its organs and biological structure let it perceive. In other words, divergent anatomies give rise to divergent worlds. Rather than a single world shared among the different types of bodies, there are different types of worlds, insofar as each type of creature is sensitized to certain types of environmental elements that are significant to it according to its specific modes of habitation. Thus, as Cassirer (1944) would say, in the world of a fly we find only things concerning flies, just as in the world of a sea urchin we find only things concerning sea urchins. These worlds are surrounded by elements in which an animal's bearers of signification move. What their senses can perceive is not the same as for other types of organisms; each one has a world that is meaningful to it. Thus, the tick—to take one of Uexküll's examples—is particularly sensitive to butyric acid, which is found on mammalian skin. Of all the environmental factors surrounding the tick's body, the organism and its receptors select butyric acid as the stimulus that serves as a guide for its survival.

Like the tick, each creature inhabits a different affective environment defined by the elements that are important to it and its lifestyle. Living organisms distinctively select the elements to which they become sensitive according to the possibilities offered by the place, their bodily structure, and the meanings that are useful to their immediate experience. This is why a *multiplicity* of surrounding worlds can coexist in the same space. In a meadow, the world of the grasshopper has nothing to do with the world of a cow grazing next to it, nor with the world of the flies that fly around the cow or the tick that lives in its skin, nor with the world of the shepherd who takes the cow to graze. Each world is different from the neighboring world. There are as many worlds as there are ways of being, each made up of the spectrum of components that matter to each type of organism according to its morphology and the range of activities of its peculiar way of living (Castro-García, 2009).

But these multiple worlds are not isolated: they share meanings and are linked in accordance with the capacity to inhabit among different beings. As Eugenio Trías (1991) contends, the limit imposed by each world does not only fence and differentiate it; its function is not only to demarcate borders. The boundary also allows for contact and facilitates the union. Worlds are among other worlds, interpenetrating each other like soap bubbles (Castro-García, 2009). Ecosystemic self-organization depends on the interdependencies of the different worlds. Bees, for example, are attracted by the ultraviolet reflectance coming from flowers. This way, the flowers attract pollinators to ensure their reproduction, while the bees can feed. This is an encounter between the bee and the flower, a back-and-forth of worlds, a dance between the bee and the flower. As Francisco Varela (2004) says, paraphrasing Francis Huxley: the bee imagines the flower and the flower imagines the bee. They are united in such a way that both would disappear if one were removed.

Worlds among worlds means that there is difference and interdependence. There is a multiplicity of worlds or *umwelten* that interconnect according to functional circles and historical processes of dynamic coupling. There are encounters not only of bodies, but of different surrounding worlds that intertwine and link in such a way that we can say that life is in itself a *multiworld*, a world formed by multiple connecting worlds, which in their process of meeting in the biosphere layer are shaping the proportions and patterns of our living planet's beauty.

Human Alterity in the Web of Life

According to Geertz's anthropology (1991), human beings are a singular type of creature that weaves its life thanks to symbolic formations. But this must be understood as a defining quality of our species in the paths that we form together with others. Our body, in its forms of "being," affects and is affected by contact with other manifestations of life in the world. But these affections, as Emma León (2017) explains so well, are fused and confused between chemical, thermal, and electrical energies and mental processes. Encounters affect us, but in an amalgamated way in which contact, perception, consciousness, unconsciousness, cravings, desires, and feelings merge. These elements are activated during the exchange with other incarnations, creatures, and forces. We integrate these affections into our body, and together they influence the interwoven tapestry of sensitivities.

We endow with meaning this magma of affections—which sometimes translate into joy, tenderness, love, pleasure, or compassion, and at other times into repulsion, hostility, hatred, envy, contempt, indignation, anger, or anguish. These affections are embodied within us, and we imprint meaning on them through words, thought, and reason. This is how we organize them in language. Our territory-body is a multiplicity of materials, affections, and cohesive contents that move us, that create sentimental eruptions—according to León's insightful concept—and that are in constant renewal. Their possibilities are associated with our long phylogenetic and social history, and thus differ from other types of phylogenetic and social trajectories (Leon, 2017).

The collective human becoming shapes and molds this maelstrom of affections through its cultural complex. We use our rational capacities and our "understanding to give meaning or purpose to our moods and feelings" (León, 2017, p. 152). We use language to shape our emotional disturbances and reactions that arise as a result of being among other bodies. We have no other refuge than to render in language, according to our cultural possibilities, the flow of forces that meet each other.

To better understand this intertwining of mental states, the bodies we interact with, and linguistic forms, it is useful to consider the example of color perception. Neurobiologist Francisco Varela (2000) has explained how perception does not consist in "recovering" the "information" that arrives from the outside in a precise manner—as conceived by positivist epistemology. Color is in fact a kind of encounter, a phylogenetic dialogue that activates one mode of association among many others that may be possible depending on each organism's coevolutionary history. Varela (2000) points out how light and reflection create a disturbance that activates neural networks to create sensory-motor correlations. It is thanks to the history of each organism—think of the difference in color worlds between a human being and the bee mentioned above, for example—that a mode of association or encounter between bodies or worlds becomes regular and repetitive. Thus, for linguistic convenience we can imagine that colors correspond to or represent some aspects of the world, when in fact they are the emergence of an encounter between a world outside the organism that triggers other internal encounters, such as cooperative neuronal operations (Varela, 2000).

However, the capabilities of the human body and its cognitive ability to signify a type of world is not a pan-human universal. While there are regularities in color perception specific to the species, there are chromatic perceptions specific to each culture's language. The perception of "yellow," "blue," "red," "black," or "white" in English is not the same as the perception of those same "colors" in New Guinean Dani, a language with only two terms for the basic colors. The perception of "green" and "blue" in Spanish is not the same as in Tarahumara, a language with only one term for green and blue. To a large extent, chromatic memory is a function of each culture's linguistic designations. This example shows how perception is in fact an encounter that depends on our biological and cultural history and on the combination of each species' long coevolutionary trajectory and each culture's specific social trajectory (Varela, Thompson, and Rosch, 1997). Surrounding worlds or *umwelten* differ not only among creatures of different species. There are different types of worlds within the same species, which vary according to their actions and needs.

The inhabited world is also the world of our desires, a world governed by complex pathways at different scales, where aspects of the biology and physiology of each type of organism are combined with language and culturally differentiated worlds. Inhabiting escapes any kind of dichotomy between the rational and the affective, the mind and the rest of the body, the conscious and the unconscious, and nature and culture. We are exchanging among bodies in a field of forces where all kinds of dualism are diluted. We are symbolic-biotic-affective bodies, in Patricia Noguera's terminology (2012), that is, bodies in which complex sentimental elaborations are nestled, infiltrated by social linguistic entanglements and collective forms of enunciation. We are the intertwining fire, air, earth, and water, the stardust of the constellations, with moods and temperaments, words and affections, and desire and power, in a pattern of dynamic and impermanent self-organization.

Neither human beings nor any other creature is enclosed within themselves, imprisoned in the capsule of their skin; instead we are passengers on a journey that we make together, which seems to begin at birth and end at death, but which is actually a much longer journey of constant transformations and unimagined trajectories through which we wander across different scales and times. We contrast the concepts of life and death in another dualism, when they are actually part of the same process of becoming *multiplicities*, of being entities in constant transformation. Death seems to be the end of life. It just happens, like a switch that suddenly turns off. But death is another process of the continuity of being here, of being a mode of emergence and manifestation of the immanence of life, and of obeying the universe's processes of constant recycling of matter, energy transformation, and entropy. However, as symbolic-biotic-affective beings we must give a kind of meaning to what we call death and what we call life through language. As moderns, we historicize the former with scientific jargon; the latter, more elusive and inscrutable, we symbolize with the invocation of the sacred and the divine. In any of its forms we are storifying anguish, uncertainty, fear, and "the question of the meaning of being"—in Heideggerian terms—through language. We are therefore inseparable aggregates between matter and symbol: a very transitory and short becoming which experiences its brief "individual" state through a linguistic format.

Environmental *Ethos*

Environmental epistemo-aesthesis is more than a way of understanding how the thought and heart of a presumptuous and confused culture dissociated and strayed from the earth that we are. It is an ontology of life which attempts to reintegrate the understanding of our earthly sojourn to the immeasurability of the universe. To do so, it tries to break all anthropocentric molds to create another form of symbolic coupling which is part of a new *ethos*—a word that originally designates the place to live. More than an epistemology, this way of understanding our ways of being and Inhabiting is an epistemo-aesthesis—as philosopher Patricia Noguera would say—replacing the suffix "logos" by "aesthesis," understood as the intensity of sensory perceptions. In it, as we have seen, there is a dissolution of the modern subject and object. This avoids starting from false dichotomies in favor of starting with the body itself and the way we are affected by the different encounters. Here the discussions about monisms or dualisms cease to make much sense, opening the way to involvement, to being in here among *multiplicities*.

The ethics that emerges from this environmental epistemo-aesthesis is not a moral "ought." Morality is not the point of view of the being among bodies. It is the system of judgment which functions through values, precepts, and mandates. In the *Tao te king* it is very well understood when it is said: "when the Tao disappears, morality appears." When the sense of belonging to an all-encompassing whole disappears, the need to tell others what they "ought" to do arises and obligation and rational judgment emerges. Environmental ethics, on the other hand, is based on an ontology of being, the ontology of inhabiting: "it is closer to wisdom than to reason" (Varela, 1992, p. 13). What should we tell others? Not to cut down forests? Not to pollute? To take care of water? None of this. We do not have any kind of imperative, nothing that we understand better, no kind of moral superiority. We start from another geography, from the geo-graphy of contact (Noguera, 2012).

The environmental *ethos* is based on contact with the beings of the world and the awareness of what this contact entails. It starts with the involvement of the body itself, from the immediate confrontation with situations of which we become aware (Varela, 1992), as when we pay attention to the movement of the apple and the paths it follows until it touches the surface of our tongue. In this way we become aware of the encounters, and in the end we understand ourselves as inter-corporealities. It is not an epistemology of transcendental metaphysics in which we start from an external world about which we arrive with rational judgments, but we do it including our participation, our sensible universe; including our own body. It is not about seeking blame or "feeling bad." On the contrary, it is about appreciating ourselves engaged in the pleasures of "Being," knowing that we are inter-penetrated in each breath with the bodies and recognizing how pleasurable the relationship with the beings of the world is (Grosso, 2012).

Becoming sensitive to the phenomenology of encounters entails recognizing when "I feel good," when the encounter with the other gives me joy, to the extent that the other bodies combine with my body in favorable proportions and conditions; when the power of a body, its force, its energy, and its magnetism, mixes with mine in such a way that I experience pleasure; but also when the encounters generate unpleasant experiences for me, when the encounter between two bodies occurs in such a way that I feel bad, I feel sadness, indignation, and anger (Deleuze, 1978). Both are sensitive experiences that affect me, and they enhance a certain way of acting. Perhaps this way we can feel joy at the encounters between our bodies and the bodies of a place overflowing with relationships, and we can feel sadness at the devastation of life.

Inter-corporeal entanglement generates affections. "We are affected," which means that our body has an effect by the action of another body. This, of course, cannot be done at a distance: it involves contact, an interwoven combination of bodies, a contact that affects one body, and that body another, and so on, creating a mixture of bodies. However, it is and will remain a mystery how things are made present in experience and how affections and mental processes come to life. We have no idea how the bodies are mixed. We only have sensitivity to know it: we know other bodies by the affections they produce in our bodies. I can only know the knots, the interwoven paths, the meshes of bodies, and myself, through the action that other bodies exert on mine. I cannot know the sun itself except by its effect on my body, by how that body modifies me, by how its rays merge with the characteristic relations of my own body.

The environmental *ethos* is thus an epistemo-aesthesis. It is a way in which sensitivities, the sentient, the felt, the skin, and the contacts come into the scene (Noguera, 2004). It is an ethic that always starts from the body. We follow Spinozian ethics, which is not based on values and moral judgments, but on an active ethics that asks, what can a body do? That is, we do not ask, what do you ought to do?, but what are you capable of? What can you do? It is not a question for an abstract body, but a question addressed to me: what is it that I can do, what experience am I capable of, what can I do by virtue of my potency? (Deleuze, 1978). This ethic is active, it speaks to us of power, of the things we are capable of when we recognize ourselves as bodies among bodies, and of the power that we have when we know ourselves as a mode or expression of an enveloping totality.

And who can awaken to the power of their body? Those who, through their own affective experience, have confidence in the exuberance of life and intuit that their body is much more than a solitary body enclosed in the capsule of the skin. On the contrary, they know themselves to be in excess, in overabundance. Those who perceive that life gives us much more than that can be taken from it, more than that can be accumulated. Those who understand that what comes from the confluence of multiple inflows must be dispersed at the risk of becoming destructive (Bataille, 1987). This is an attitude toward life that requires exercise and practice. Those who do not know it, although they are interconnected, interrelated, and interdependent like everyone else, live their body as selfhood, in a shortage of relationships, and therefore experience impotence and passivity. Overwhelmed by passive affections, their capacity is reduced to its minimum expression. The power of the body is known in the open exposure to the world, in the offering to other beings, in a centrifugal power of acting which dissipates and distributes instead of accumulating and hoarding for itself. This relational ontology expresses itself ethically by a kind of trust and faith in the generosity of life (Mandoki, 2013), according to which we can give in exuberance, since in some way or another it will be recovered because we are the mode, the expression of something much greater, a body inhabited and inhabiting among *multiplicities*.

This ethics arises as a correlate of an ontology of inter-being. As long as we do not begin with the body, and we do not know what its power is, it will be very difficult to channel the wisdom necessary to redirect the social order to the order of life. The goal is to explore the possibilities of what our body, *your body*, *my body*, can do, and to inquire into its potency. But it is a potency in the action. The goal is to experience our capacity, not our duty. Unlike morality, in which we learn rules that we must obey—the biblical commandments, the father's orders, the law—or face punishment—the final judgment, beating by belt, prison—it is a potential act that arises from the ontological understanding of our constitution as bodies among bodies, from our composition as beings made of relationships. In the end, this ethic has to do with awakening to the power of one's own body, to exercise the power we are potentially capable of.

This is certainly not easy. As Francisco Varela (1992, p. 42) says, "the world we live in is so close at hand that we do not ponder what it is or how we live in it." Our daily encounters with the beings of the world with whom we interpenetrate seem so given that not only do we not see them, but we do not see that we do not see them, as Varela assures. The challenge then is finding different doors to exercise sensitivity until we discover that we are bodies among bodies, worlds among worlds, and the result of multiple encounters of skins: inter-beings inter-being. There is no way out but to appeal to the wisdom and power of our body, to co-construct together this other *ethos* if we want to turn around the civilizational collapse we are headed toward. Dichotomies have no place in this goal. We need an epistemo-aesthesis that brings out a different kind of sensitivity, one that empowers us to reinscribe our actions in the conditions that make life on Earth possible.

2

Beings Corporealizing Next to Others: Environmental Empathy

We ended the first chapter saying that environmental ethics and the practical implications for environmental learning will continue to be misguided if they are mistaken for moral dictates, mandates, or recommendations. Environmental ethics is quite different: it needs to start with the exploration of the body's capabilities; it requires starting from affections, feelings, sentience, and contact; it needs to assemble the power that emerges from being affected by contact with the world's sentient beings. As we have said, the great problem of the environmental crisis originates in modern dualisms, in thought that is detached from the conditions that make life possible. Yet it is more than an epistemic issue; the problem delves to the deepest foundations of our body; it reaches the intimacy of our entrails, our minds, our skin, and the sensory-motor potentialities of our constitution as symbolic-biotic bodies (Noguera, 2012). The orientation of desire to the empire of commodities and the concomitant insensitivity to the presence of other bodies is perhaps the greatest tragedy of our times. Hence the urgent need to ask ourselves about what our body can do, about the possibility of an environmental way of thinking that prioritizes the sentient universe, the senses, and affections.

We are thinking of an ethics that, rather than being enunciated, is discovered by exploring the body. We believe that much of the theoretical-methodological-aesthetic inquiry (Noguera, Ramírez, and Echeverry, 2020) of this pathway can be rooted in the phenomenological tradition, in the recent enactive perspective of neurocognition, and in environmental empathy. The purpose is to address some debates that we consider important for going a little further in our understanding of these questions: What can a body do? Who knows its power? What background is necessary for cultivating bodily capacity and for potency to emerge?

The core of our argument is that cultivating empathy makes it possible to experience one's own living body as interrelated with the other bodies we inhabit with. The problem of modern capitalism and its structures of meaning is that it prevents us from having empathic openness, empathic contagion, and exploration of the emotions and potencies related to the other human and non-human beings we coexist with. Other bodies are thought of as objects, as things, as available resources, as useful services, and as something that is placed in front of us in the form of an externality. The dissociation of *multiplicities* into two orders—the human on the one hand, and nature as a thing on the other hand—is possible because the sentimental capacities are not cultivated, and therefore the body loses power. Its power to act in the face of ecocide diminishes. Being sensitive, cultivating environmental sensitivity, means being guided by the experience of other bodies and valuing the feelings and emotions of others.

Without environmental sensitivity, without the empathic contagion, without the exploration of emotionality that arises from our capacity to be affected by the emotion of other bodies, we cannot do ethics and we must resort to morality, to rational judgment, to the legislated duties of law. This is why empathy as a trigger of affections associated with anger, indignation, guilt, shame, or joy is a prerequisite for environmental ethics. This ethic is relative, flexible, and contextual, without categories of good and evil that can be adopted generally or reduced to axioms applied universally.

We will begin with a phenomenological discussion of cognition, perception, and affections, and then we will address empathy and inter-corporeal relations between humans and other beings. We will discuss the affective possibilities that arise from our capacity as empathic beings, and at the end of the chapter we will discuss how we are heirs to a common language in which, like communicating vessels, we weave life through inter-sensitive wefts.

Enactive Approach to Neurocognition

Starting with the body and what it is capable of can lead us to an analysis of the cognitive and mental capacities of our constitution as biological beings. We believe that this avenue opens a field of possibilities for environmental thought in terms of our epistemic-aesthetic considerations about bodies among bodies and encounters. It also helps us understand the biological bases of intercorporeality and environmental knowledge based on affectivity. In particular, we would like to rely on the enactive[1] approach to neurobiology, a line of research that for several years has been drawing on the contributions of Husserlian, Merleupontian, and Heideggerian phenomenological philosophy for studying cognition and the brain.

In general terms, neurophenomenology—as Francisco Varela named it—rejects the idea that the mind is housed in the cranial vault and the assertion that its function is to properly represent the external world. According to this approach, the mind does not operate by collecting data from an external environment, nor can its task be conceived as the passive reception of information. On the contrary, the mind extends throughout the body and includes the world beyond the organism (Thompson, 2010). In the words of Andy Clark (1999, p. 93): "The mind is an elusive organ that constantly slips out of its 'natural' confines and blatantly mingles with the body and the world." Thus, rather than apprehending the characteristics of the external environment reliably, the mind's function is to creatively signify the rest of the bodies among which we are to inhabit a shared world.

We must recall that the phenomenological school makes a radical critique of the deep-rooted belief that the understanding of the world is independent of the knower, that everything exists without the participation of the observer, and that reality "is there," independent of the experience of the perceiver. Phenomenology holds instead that reality arises dependent on the perceiver; bodies are not separate from other bodies; they have always been in relation to the world. Maurice Merleau-Ponty (1957) said that our body is in the world as the heart is in the organism: it forms a system with it. The human body, like the bodies of all creatures, is embedded in the world, interacting with each of its components. In fact, there would be no space for me if I had no body. My body is the perspective from which I interact with the world and the place from which I perceive everything else. It is the point of reference with respect to which all other entities are related. This means that we are embodied and situated agents. It is from "my here," from the proprioceptive sense of my own body in space—the biological ability to know where my feet are in relation to the floor, my arms in relation to the desk, or my whole body in relation to other things—that I can experience the world and interact with it.

Neurophenomenology revisits these discussions by paying attention to an aspect that phenomenological philosophy has emphasized for more than a century: the idea that we are embodied beings, that we inhabit in and through a body. In this sense our actions, perceptions, and ways of inhabiting depend on our bodily existence. The body is the constitutive principle because it holds the very possibility of experience. Our relationship with the world, with others, and with ourselves depends on what the body "can," its capacity (Gallagher and Zahavi, 2014). One of the implications of the embodied perspective is that, for a mind to exist, the body must actively manipulate and interact with the world. In other words, the world is not separate from us, nor are we spectators who perceive the world from within, but instead the world is always co-emerging as the fruit of our activity.

It is easier to grasp this seemingly abstract idea with the example of a classic experiment by Held and Hein (1958) cited by Varela (2000). As you may know, cats are born blind and open their eyes within the first eight to ten days after birth. In a 1958 experiment, two groups of newborn kittens were placed in different baskets in a darkened room. Cats in the first group could walk normally but were tied to a carousel with a basket that carried cats from the second group, who could not move. The two groups of cats had the same visual experience, but the second group was totally passive. Once the cats were released and exposed to the light, the group that had moved behaved normally, but the group that had remained stationary did not recognize objects, tripped, and fell down the stairs. It was as if they were blind cats, even though their eyes were intact. The phenomenological conclusion of this experiment is that space arises as a product of motion. Indeed, the space existed for the walking cat, because they had interacted with it by walking, but for the cats in the second group there was no space beyond their basket, because they would have had to manipulate it first with their own sensory-motor behavior (Varela, 2000). As this example shows, space is not a container that surrounds us, but rather an environment shaped by our senses and bodies in motion (Thompson, 2010).

Another experiment that shows that cognition is produced by interacting with the environment is in the research of Walter Freeman (1975), who inserted electrodes into a rabbit's olfactory bulb.[2] His main finding is that "there is no pattern of activity in the bulb unless the animal is exposed to a specific smell several times" (Varela, Thompson, and Rosch, 1997, p. 205). In other words, the rabbit cannot have an olfactory experience if it has not been repeatedly exposed to a type of smell beforehand. This conclusion shows that smell is not the retrieval of the external features of objects. It involves a form of meaningful creativity based on the animal's history. Smell is an act in which the recognition of the scent as a felt and experienced smell is constrained by experience and by the intentions of the present moment.

Color, as discussed in the previous chapter, is another example that supports the neurophenomenological approach. It has been shown (Land, 1977) that the sensation of color is independent of the wavelength of the light reflected by a body. When green is viewed in isolation, for example, it reflects a high percentage of medium-wave light back to the eye, and a low percentage of long—and short-wave light. However, when the color is viewed as part of a complex scene, it will still feel green even if it reflects more long waves and short waves than medium waves (Varela, Thompson, and Rosch, 1997). In other words, color perception does not match the measurement standards of science. In reality, color is not found in the wavelengths of light. Just think of how a dog, a dragonfly, or an octopus would apprehend color. Color, rather than expressing the luminous qualities of an object, is a symbiosis between the organism and the world (Varela, 2000); it is an intertwining that depends on evolutionary history and linguistic communities. The perception of color cannot be explained as the correct representation of an external world, but instead depends on the capabilities of phylogenetic, ontogenetic, and cultural history—in what "each body can," in Spinoza's terminology—as well as on the place and the possibilities that a specific environment offers. Cognition is the act of a body interacting among other bodies, an assemblage of relationships where the brain, the senses, and the other bodies that inhabit the universe interconnect.

The cases described above teach us that to inhabit a place is not to passively be in a physical space, but to be in an active relationship with meaningful circumstances, carrying out actions in specific contexts. The olfactory world of the rabbit, its *umwelt*, is not the same as the mouse's, and not even the same as that of a rabbit that lives in a totally different space, just as our visual perception is not the same as the fly's. Each world depends on the bodies' history of interaction with the components of the inhabited place. To paraphrase Gallagher and Zahavi (2014), the possibilities that each body allows for, but also those that they prevent or limit, define space as a world of permissibilities, as situations of meaning and circumstances for action, just as the inhabited space determines the corporeal forms for the body to interact with the place and be included in it. Cognition means responding to an element that affects me, and as we see in the case of odor, it presupposes a previous affectation, a previous disturbance. The perception of textures, sounds, flavors, the visual field, or aromas is informed by past experiences, by intentionalities, and also by feelings, mood, and all the specific aspects of my individual, social, and biological history that shape my corporeality and define how I perceive the world. In perceiving the world, whatever is salient to me must have affected me, it must have created an affective force that becomes relevant to the extent that it captures my attention (Gallagher and Zahavi, 2014).

What are the implications for environmental thought of the enactive perspective of cognition? We have been arguing that the environment could well be imagined as a zone of encounters between different kinds of bodies and worlds, which are not random, but intertwine following aesthetic patterns. The "environmental" is the result of encounters between *multiplicities* of skins. However, we can now go a step further because these encounters affect me in the sense that they corporealize me by adopting the affections, sensibilities, feelings, sensations, and impulses of the space my body inhabits. But space is also the product of the affections and affects that arise from the actions that different types of bodies perform on each other, including my own. Enactive cognition is therefore implication, intertwining between the affective states of our own body, as well as the affective state of the place. This is another way of saying that places also feel since they are receptacles of the affections, sensitivities, affects, and feelings of the bodies that comprise them.

Cézanne said that color is the place where our brain and the universe meet. Now we can say that not only color but also smell, sounds, flavors, and tactile experience are encounters that fold, unfold, and refold, where diverse universes of bodies come together, where the affections and atmospheres of places merge with the materiality, chemistry, and energetic flows of our diverse corporeal expressions. Cognition is not a matter of my enclosed brain acting on a network of neurons, but a matter of sensitivity, feelings, and affections between different types of bodies that meet: my body and the sensitivity of the air-body that I breathe, the water-body that I drink and exude, the ground-body that I step on and supports me, and the landscape-body composed of different types of bodies.

Those sensitivities that occur in the tangle of encounters induce our action. In a way, encounters are something we do because we have bodily abilities. But at the same time they are something that happens to us, something that affects us and induces our action. As Emmanuel Levinas would say, the presence of other bodies is imposed on us. It is not a matter of choice, but instead it emerges independently of our will, without any freedom of choice. The sensory experience of the river, the mountain, the animals, the floor, the trees, and the people who inhabit them is imposed from the outside and is present without us having to exert any mental effort (Myin and O'Regan, 2002). We are together with others, but my possibilities of experience are limited to my sensory-motor skills and the characteristics of the inhabited place, and by the emergent capacity of these encounters to trigger action.

The neurophenomenological approach teaches us that the mind is not separate from the world. Instead what we experience, think, and feel is emerging as a result of our activity. We are beings in movement. We are becomings intertwining with other bodies, molding the space with our bodies and sensory-motor skills, and we get to know the world through the process of interacting with other bodies. Therefore, the presence of other bodies, on the one hand, is imposed on us without any possibility of choice, but, on the other hand, we are active inhabitants moving, touching, listening, smelling, tasting, allowing ourselves to be affected, and performing actions in the inhabited place.

What then can a body do? My body? This depends on my possibilities of experience, which, as we have seen, are not an individual property. At every moment they are being created through a dialectic between what is mine and what is not, between self and other, through the recognition of the continuous dependence on otherness, which means accepting that the other inhabits my self. Environmental ethics implies a decentering of selfhood, openness to the world, and the affectation produced by proximity to other bodies. In Levinas' terminology, to be ethical (1987) *is to be affected by the other*; it is to let oneself be touched in emotion, in sensitivity to the fact of inhabiting together; and in addition to sensitivity, it is to use our cognition to creatively signify the phenomenology of encounters. As we will see later, this signification depends to a large extent on our ability to combine our capacity to recognize the affectivity of our intercorporeal intertwining with linguistic, ritual, and technical elements specific to each culture.

Empathy and Affective Connection between Bodies

In what sense are my emotions, my affections, my mind, and the world outside my body intimately involved? In what way are the sensory and motor systems specific to my human body sensitively linked to the affections of other bodies that inhabit me and which I inhabit? We would like to address these questions through the beautiful tale *The Joy of Fishes* by Zhuang Zhou (369–290 BC):

> Zhuang Zhou and Hui Shi were crossing the Hao River by the dam.
> Zhuang Zhou said,
> See how freely the fish jump and run. That is their joy.

Hui Shi replied,
"Since you are not a fish, how can you know what makes fish joyful?"
Zhuang Zhou said:
"Since you are not me, how can you possibly know that I do not know what makes fish joyful?" Hui Shi argued:
"If I, not being you, cannot know what you know, it is evident that you, not being a fish, cannot know what they know."
Zhuang Zhou said:
"Wait a minute! Let us go back to the original question. You asked me how I can know what makes fish joyful. From the way you posed the question, you obviously know that I know what makes fish joyful. I know the joy of the fish in the river through my own joy as I walk along the same river."

What does it mean to feel the joy of the fish through my own joy? Much of the recent discussion in psychology, neuroscience, anthropology, and sociology on this topic has been based on the concept of empathy, defined as the capacity of our species to engage dynamically with the emotionality of others (Thompson, 2001). It has been said that empathy is the capacity to feel touched in emotion by the emotion of the other. When this capacity is cultivated, as in Zhuang Zhou's story, it can affect us in such a way that we can feel joy when fish feel joy or sadness when fish feel sadness. In other words, we understand that we are interpellated by the presence of the other and the situation they are living in.

Empathy is a biological capacity that is not exclusive to our species. Primatologist Frans de Waal (2011) asserts that empathy is a trait we share with other animal species. De Waal (2011) analyzes scientific research and experiments that study such things as the behavior of chimpanzees, capuchins, bonobos, mice, dolphins, and elephants, and concludes that many actions of these animals show concern for the welfare of their fellow animals.[3] In particular, higher primates, including humans, have a very particular capacity deep in our genes: the ability to interpret the other's state of mind. We can attribute intentionality to their actions and become emotionally infected by their situation, never losing the distinction that their experience is not our own (Thompson, 2001, 2005).

Empathy is a fundamental part of the evolutionary process of our mammalian lineage, and it involves brain areas that are more than one hundred million years old (De Waal, 2011). This biological apparatus formed during the cognitive and affective process of hominization allows us to respond and function in contexts with social encounters (Morin, 1971). Our capacity for empathy is rooted in the phylogenetic history of our biological body, making it possible for us to fulfill the social relationship. It is so innate that newborn babies, in some cases less than an hour old, can imitate the facial gestures of another person. This shows the congenital ability to match the facial movements of others with their own body, that is, to use the proprioceptive awareness of their own face to copy the gestures of another (Meltzoff and Moore, 1977). Peñaranda (2010) links empathic recognition with the neonate's evolutionary need to be cared for and protected to survive. In fact, Csibra and Gergely (2009) have described the greater likelihood that the infant will imitate gestures if the other person pays attention to them. Empathy, from the enactive approach, reminds us that our biological and evolutionary history has developed a genetic endowment to develop our life in radical coexistence with others we depend on to exist. In this sense empathy is not a passive observation but a perception for interaction.

This biological stickiness characteristic of our primate makeup has been associated with the discovery of "mirror neurons," a particular type of neurons that activate when we observe or imagine the behavior performed by another person, or when we are preparing to imitate the same action (Rizzolatti and Craighero, 2004). Mirror neurons show how the motor system is activated as if we were performing the observed action and how our body resonates from the encounter with the other.[4] Our body "can" respond to the emotions of others by adopting a congruent emotion, that is, by emotionally attuning to the action, gesture, posture, or intention of another person. If I perceive joy, anger, fear, or disgust, my body can tune in to and resonate with the emotion, although always recognizing that it is not actually "my emotion," but an external emotion I can connect with (Gallagher and Zahavi, 2014).

In reality, the other person's body always appears to me as radically different. The experience of emotional contagion does not mean that we reproduce the same emotion as the other; empathy is about the fact that other people's emotions awaken our own. Gallagher and Zahavi (2014) argue that there is something in the other's affectivity that we can experience directly, as emotions always occur in meaningful contexts that are co-determined by the action and expression of the body. Thus we can perceive joy in the other person when they smile, sadness in their tears, embarrassment when they blush, or anger in their frown. Thanks to empathy, we experience the other person face to face as someone whose bodily gestures or actions are expressing their mental states. However, the authors continue, this does not mean that we can feel exactly what the other feels. That is only possible for the person who is happy, sad, embarrassed, or angry. We can perceive these moods and expressive movements but not in the same way as the person experiencing them. If it were the same experience as mine, the other would cease to be otherness and would begin to be part of myself. So, on the one hand, I can directly experience the other because we are constant interpreters of the mental and psychic state of our fellow humans, but, on the other hand, there is something elusive and inaccessible in their experience. There are certainly situations in which we would have no reason to doubt that the other is feeling pain, anger, or boredom. But there are also situations in which we do not have access to the other's emotion and therefore must find out how they are feeling (Gallagher and Zahavi, 2014). Empathy is largely explained by the fact that there is never an isolated experience; they are always part of a context. A gesture, an expression, or an action always takes place in a concrete situation. It is our understanding of the context, of what happened before, and the action that follows that helps us to connect with the other's emotion. Therefore, emotional contagion is not always enough; it is often necessary to rely on an interpretation of the context to understand what is happening. Understanding others is contextual, and therefore empathy, Gallagher and Zahavi claim, does not mean projecting oneself emotionally onto the other, but rather the ability inherent in our biological constitution to experience other minds in meaningful and practical contexts of action. In their own words, "to understand other people I must not first get inside their minds; rather, I must pay attention to the world I already share with them" (Gallagher and Zahavi, 2014, p. 285).

Empathy, however, can go beyond the simple understanding of the other's emotions when the ability to understand their emotional state moves us to act in favor of their wellbeing. With a high degree of empathy we notice the fear and provide relief, we hear the child's cry and come to comfort them, or someone is about to fall and we immediately come to their aid (Vreeke and Van der Mark, 2003). In this sense, empathy is enaction, perception for ethical action. This level of empathy is called "empathic concern," an emotional response provoked by the situation experienced by the other, and which is congruent with an interest in their well-being (Batson, 2009). Varela (1992) calls this ethic "immediate action," a pre-rational ethic in which we not only feel the body of the other person, but also value their feelings and emotions and come to their aid. Varela (2000, p. 469) takes an example cited by the Confucian Mencius (371–289 BC) to say that if I see a child standing on the edge of a well about to fall, "there is no thought, no morality: I save the child" (p. 469).

This level of empathy requires a double effort, since despite being in tune with others through a connection with their emotions, it is also necessary to put some distance from the adopted emotion. For example, if we encounter someone experiencing some kind of sadness, we can be receptive to their emotion by experiencing a similar emotion in ourselves; but if we remain feeling that sadness without any kind of distance, our ability to help and to imagine solutions will be diminished. A high level of empathy must be accompanied by "the ability to regulate emotions and control feelings" (Vreeke and Van der Mark, 2003, p. 188), since not controlling them and allowing them to overflow will reduce our ability to act responsibly toward the other, even if we have the best intentions to seek their well-being.

This conceptualization of empathy as the basic affective and cognitive capacity that underlies all feelings and emotions characteristic of ethics has been thought of mainly from the point of view of inter-human interaction. But what about ethics toward non-humans? Is it possible to develop ethics from the perspective of environmental empathy? What about the ability to empathize or share emotions with entities other than oneself?

Several recent studies in psychology (Schultz, 2002; Tam, 2013; Pfattheicher, Sassenrath, and Schindler, 2016; Sevillano, Corraliza, and Lorenzo, 2017) have developed the concept of "empathy with nature," defined as the tendency to "understand and share the emotional experience, and in particular the suffering, of the natural world" (Tam, 2013, p. 93). This tendency is shown when people feel distress upon seeing the image of a mistreated animal (Schultz, 2002) or when they are exposed to images showing the consequences of environmental devastation. However, Tam (2013) asserts that empathy with nature is different from human-to-human empathy, as it presupposes an emotional connection with nature which is not present in all people. Schultz (2002) argues that the environmental concern that people develop is closely associated with how they view themselves. When individuals tend to define themselves as relatively independent of their environment, environmental devastation does not arouse much interest in them, or, at most, there will be a concern motivated by instrumental interests. On the contrary, those who have a sense of themselves in continuity with nature, and therefore feel affectively attached to other expressions of life, tend to have higher levels of empathy with other beings. One conclusion from this research is that in the latter group there is high correspondence between empathy toward humans and empathy with nature, whereas in those who feel separate from, or above nature, human empathy is not associated with empathy toward other living beings (Tam, 2013; Sevillano et al., 2017). One of the great problems of the ontological conception of the separate-being is that empathy diminishes when other beings are not recognized as sensitive and sentient. If we consider a mountain, a forest, or a river as inert and insentient, empathy with these beings becomes unlikely. An additional problem is what Hoffman (1992) defines as "empathic bias": the fact that human beings tend to activate empathy with those we feel closest to. We tend to be partial and identify with those who have special relationships with us, with whom we feel affinity, or with beings who have physical similarities with us. It is easier to accept that we can empathize with another human being than to accept that we can feel in our own body the emotion of a mountain, a tree, a wetland, or a community of cockroaches.

There are criticisms of the empathy approach to non-human beings. Kasperbauer (2015), for example, argues that the emotions often cited in these studies may bear no resemblance to what the affected bodies may be feeling. This author points out that, when empathizing with a non-human being, there will always be a question as to whether we are really sharing their feelings or emotions, or whether we are projecting our own onto them. Kasperbauer may be right, as many of the studies thus far are associated with the theory of "perspective-taking," an approach to empathy[5] that involves imaginatively putting oneself in another's situation to surmise how one would feel in their position (Oxley, 2011). People participating in these experiments are presented with images or videos of animals affected by pollution or the destruction of their ecosystems and are asked to put themselves in their place and describe their feelings (Schultz, 2002).

The problem with "perspective-taking" is that it starts from a controversial assumption: that I only have access to my own mind. I can draw on past experiences of my own embodiment to infer that other sensitive bodies must be feeling something like what I would feel if I were in their situation. If I see a bird with a plastic bag around its neck, I associate it with an experience in which I felt suffocated, and therefore infer that the bird must be suffering. The argument is that we cannot experience the other's thoughts or feelings but only infer what they must feel based on our body's own experience. The question then becomes valid: When we imaginatively project ourselves into another's perspective, do we really understand them? Might I not simply be understanding myself? (Gallagher and Zahavi, 2014). And in the case of a tree or a rock, which are foreign bodies to me sensitively, will I be able to simulate putting myself in their situation?

This notion of empathy is problematic because it is linked to that dichotomous thinking in which an isolated body can understand another isolated body by simulating its situation. But, as we have been arguing, we are bodies among bodies. In the everyday world we do not encounter bodies as thematic objects that we can see in an image or video and then simulate and rationalize. We are-in-a-world in pragmatic, non-simulated situations. Our way of inhabiting and being with others and understanding each other is related to the concrete lived situation and to all the sensorial possibilities that my body allows for. I do not see the other only with my eyes; I meet them and they meet me; we connect through inter-sensitivities, through the conjugation of chemical substances, vibrations, and radiations. The forces that are being formed interact in different ways, conscious and unconscious, and therefore, what we feel depends on the intertwining of intercorporealities and relational entanglements. In empathy we experience the other directly as a body, as a being we live with and perceive in the immediacy of intuition, but this is determined by the influence of the territory-body that constitutes us and the territory-body in which we are.

We have said that empathy is explained by the fact that it is not an isolated experience. We cannot remove the context because empathy is always occurring in concrete situations. Our understanding of what is happening helps us engage with the sensibility of the other body. The beautiful story "The Joy of Fishes" is quite telling in this regard. It begins with Zhuang Zhou and Hui Shi crossing the river, paying attention to a shared world. And it is here that Zhuang Zhou speaks: "See how freely the fish jump and run. That is their joy," he says. Of course Hui Shi doesn't understand him and replies, "Since you are not a fish, how can you know what makes fish joyful?" Hui Shi's insight helps us understand the critique of perspective-taking: "you cannot know what makes them joyful, because you are not a fish; you can only access your own mind." However, Zhuang Zhou's response to his friend's question is an affront to the idea that we cannot know the other's state of mind. "Since you are not me, how can you possibly know that I do not know what makes fish joyful?" Zhuang Zhou is telling Hui Shi that in his very question lies the key to say that something of his experience is being perceived directly, for he knows something about his companion. Hui Shi, in turn, repeats the idea that we cannot experience the thoughts of another person, much less those of an animal, and responds: "If I, not being you, cannot know what you know, it is evident that you, not being a fish, cannot know what they know." But Zhuang Zhou, in the face of this new challenge, does not say, "if you were on this side of the river, seeing it from my perspective, you could understand that from here I can simulate putting myself in the situation that the fish are in and infer that they are joyful, because if I were swimming like them

I would be joyful too." No, his answer does not speak about taking anyone's perspective, nor of hypothesizing about the fish's emotion based on what he would feel if he were in their place. Zhuang Zhou's answer is very different: "Wait a minute! Let us go back to the original question. You asked me how I can know what makes fish joyful. From the way you posed the question, you obviously know that I know what makes fish joyful." That is, you are perceiving me in this face-to-face relationship, in my gestures, in my words, in a specific context, not imagining, simulating, or theorizing a situation. And Zhuang Zhou goes on to say, well, just as you directly experience something of me, so is my experience with the fish: "I know the joy of the fish in the river *through my own joy as I walk along the same river.*" It is thanks to my own joy, to an empathic joy that is given to me by the possibilities that my body allows for and the involvement in a context full of meaning—being sensitive to the emotion of the fish while I move along the river—that I can understand their joy.

We believe that this magnificent story holds the key for understanding environmental empathy. We have said that environmental ethics needs to begin with the geography of contact and the awareness of what this contact entails. This does not mean that we can feel exactly what the coral reef, the mangrove, or the jungle feel, nor make sentient projections on them. Rather, the idea is to learn to pay attention to a shared world in which I myself inhabit, and to connect through my own emotions with the joy of the first rain, the pain of the drought, the anguish of the fish without oxygen, the fear of the trees at the noise of the chainsaw, the anger of the mutilated mountain, but not by an anthropomorphic projection,[6] but by the emotion that arises in my own body as we care for an earth we are members of. In other words, the idea is to feel joyful if the fish are joyful, sad if the air feels sad, euphoric if the waves are euphoric. To let myself be affected is to cultivate that empathic capacity we are heirs to, and which is not exclusive to the inter-human social relationship, but which is always in emergent activity even if we are unaware of it.

The fact that we are permanently encountering and embodying ourselves implies that we are embracing the sensibilities and feelings of the place where we dwell. During the process of interpenetration of bodies among bodies, we are inhabited by the affective states of the surrounding world, often without realizing it. We said that the presence of other bodies imposes itself on us, and in this sense the joy of the fish in the river becomes present in my own body. The mind is not separate from the world, but we can now say that empathic affect is the biological ability that binds bodies together; it is the glue, the myelin, and the substance that connects our body to other bodies as we move and interact with them.

But empathy cannot be considered in isolation. It is accompanied by affections of all kinds. It is the precondition, the basis, and the conditioner for the action-motivating emotions to emerge. Thus, empathy for the pain of the felled forest can be transformed into empathic anger and indignation, emotions associated with the active collective empathic response to the transgression of a territory. But empathy can also mutate into fear and hopelessness, emotions related to avoidance (Carver and Harmon-Jones, 2009; Kasperbauer, 2015). Certainly, empathy does not always generate a positive response to defend the place. We may shut down when feeling guilt, shame, or fear, but we may also open up when feeling anger, guilt, shame, desire, or gratitude. The political response to destruction is motivated more by amalgamations of emotions triggered by empathy. Thus we can feel pain-indignation-hope that motivates us to act, but we can also enter a pain-fear-despair loop which numbs our political response.

It is important to emphasize that empathy is not always associated with action-motivating emotions. We may become inhibited depending on the shape of the sensitive network that is triggered and the sensitive intensities of our affective experience. For instance, empathic excess may cause intense pain that is not associated with an ethical response, but with disconnection, flight, or avoidance (Hoffman, 2008). Emma León (2017) holds that our drive or resistance to act in the direction of something as it attract or repels us is conditioned by the experience of the affective states that arise as a result of the immense tangle of emotions, perceptions, and sensations and our impulses to seek, require, crave, or desire. Therefore, empathy is not always associated with a compassionate action, so *environmental affectivity* is restricted by the affective tonality that runs through my body at any given time.

We must understand that empathy does not mean that we need direct contact with the world's beings to be able to act ethically. We do not need to travel to the Amazon to empathize with it and become affected by the destruction of the rainforest and its inhabitants. The point is to cultivate my own sensitivity, to learn through attention how my body receives the action of other bodies and the nature of the sensitive effect I experience as the other body changes mine. Therefore, this ethic always requires contact, an awareness of the blending bodies, and learning how my affected body welcomes the traces of the affecting body. This cultivation of "myself as other" can develop our empathic capacities so that we can act by extension. Francisco Varela (1992, p. 45) states that "we acquire ethical behavior in the same way as other behaviors: all of them become imperceptible to us as we grow up in our society," and therefore, it is a matter of confronting our ethical actions in a pre-rational way and extending them to other behaviors. Varela quotes Mencius to say—as we mentioned before—that when a child is about to fall into a well, someone will surely feel compassion and come to the rescue. The ethics of the Confucian Mencius consist of extending the feelings that arise in these situations to different situations. To do so, it is enough to realize that one situation resembles another, so that feelings burst into the new situation.

Thus, it is not necessary to go to every corner of the world to act ethically as a product of empathy.

Neo-Confucian philosopher Wang Yang Ming (1472–1529), inspired by Mencius, expanded the logic of extension of empathy to compassion for all beings:

> When a man sees a child about to fall into a well, he cannot help a feeling of alarm and commiseration. This shows that his humanity forms one body with the child. It may be objected that the child belongs to the same species. Again, when he observes the pitiful cries and frightened appearance of birds and animals about to be slaughtered, he cannot help feeling an "inability to bear" their suffering. This shows that his humanity forms one body with birds and animals. It may be objected that birds and animals are sentient beings as he is. But when he sees plants broken and destroyed, he cannot help a feeling of pity. This shows that his humanity forms one body with plants. It may be said that plants are living things as he is. Yet, even when he sees tiles and stones shattered and crushed, he cannot help a feeling of regret. This shows that his humanity forms one body with tiles and stones. This means that even the mind of the small man necessarily has the humanity that forms one body with all.
>
> (Wang, 1963, p. 272)

Now the idea of an ethics that starts in the body and the ontological importance of recognizing ourselves as bodies among other bodies have become clearer. The body "can" feel "part of," "emergence from," "being with," and "being affected by" the sensibility of other bodies. But to say "can" means merely a potentiality. Empathy is the affective ability inherent in our hominid makeup, a natural disposition we are born with, an innate capacity we are naturally endowed with that we have inherited over the course of our evolutionary history. However, this does not mean that empathy is automatic and independent of the context and cultural environments in which people participate.

As anthropologist Tim Ingold (2008, p. 14) puts it: "whatever the environmental conditions, there are certain things that humans can potentially do," such as the human ability to walk upright on two feet. In the same way empathy, rather than an innate determination, is a biological potentiality that will tend to express itself if the necessary environmental conditions are present.[7] Empathy is neither an exclusively biological property nor a wholly cultural one. Rather, it arises in the inexorable encounter between our biological potential and our social and cultural environment, in the interweaving of *multiplicities*. The conjugation of these elements shapes the empathic emergence as the result of permanent feedback between internal and external factors. This is just a way of saying that empathy is neither outside nor inside. It does not depend on an environment independent of corporeality, nor can it be specified internally as a prior innate programming independent of context. Instead, we speak of a biological structure with certain potentialities, which together with an adequate environment can enable the co-emergence and development of the human capacity to feel empathy and act ethically. Empathy is a capacity that may or may not emerge experientially, and it all depends on the specific environment that enhances or inhibits biological potentialities.

"One is not born a woman," said Simone de Beauvoir (1981). In reality, one is not born anything in particular. One is born with potentialities, but for these potentials to develop they must be accompanied by the conditions necessary for their expression. The capacity for empathy, like all other human capacities, is inseparable from our body, our language, and our social history. It is rooted in our biological structure, although it is developed and experienced within a cultural background. This understanding of empathy means choosing a middle path: empathy is not "out there," separate from our bodily endowment, and neither is it "in here," independent of our cultural environment. It is tied to biology and culture, and therefore emerges in the process of mutual specification. A clear example of this association is the use of words. We experience the world according to the words we use. As we will see later, some groups were stripped of solid words that gave them a firm basis for affective interaction. The words were resignified and emptied of content, and empathy was gradually inhibited (Poerksen, 1995). On the other hand, to caress with words, to sweetly render in language, implies a different form of sensitive relationship with the beings of the world, one that is essential for the purposes of our affective cognition.

This is where the Spinozian political project that inspires us to ask ourselves what the best environment is for effecting our potency makes a lot of sense. This potency to act depends on the exploration of our own body and results in an ethics that is discovered, as in Wang Yang Ming's marvelous quote. What are the conditions that we must generate for empathy to emerge and for the body to develop its full power? What are the pragmatic and contextual activities necessary so that affection for the earth can emerge? We believe that cultivating empathy is fundamental as the detonating element of the sentient structure, human emotionalism, and the ethical response to the destruction of life. Empathy is the precondition for our experience of inhabiting a shared world, insofar as it provides that sensitive orientation which in South African *Ubuntu* is expressed with great beauty: "I am because we are."

The Earth Empathizing with Us

Merleau-Ponty's phenomenology (1968) taught us that I am felt by being inter-penetrated in a world full of others, so that when I touch the stone, I am being touched by it at the same time; when I smell a space, there are more beings sensitive to my aroma at the same time; when I see a place, I am simultaneously visible to the other bodies.

This is simply a way to say that we are only a tiny part of a sensitive universe made up of many sentient beings that sense each other. Is not just us who have the capacity to empathize with the world. The trees, the mountains, and the oceans empathize with our emotions and feelings by forming an inter-sensitive web in which all creatures in some way feel what others are feeling.

The living world surrounds us is a web of many sentient bodies that experience affections when they encounter each other. If we walk attentively through a forest, for example, we can sharpen our senses and notice how the trees look at us, how the birds hear us, how the buzzing insects flying around us or the stones we step on as we walk are able to feel us according to their peculiar way of being and the possibilities allowed for by each type of corporeality. All beings in contact, the vital forms connect our senses by combining through smells, sounds, sights, touch, taste, and all those senses characteristic of each creature's *umwelt*. The modes of existence have coevolved and transformed with us in such a way that their senses and sensations, their way of affecting and being affected, are intertwined in my body as I walk through the forest, in a dynamic coupling in which my body and the different corporealities meet.

As we have insisted, the environment is much more than the passive, inert background of modern ontology. It is, instead, the space-time where the relation between sensitive beings takes place; it is an active world in which I am present-with-others, and in which other bodies call me, know me, speak to me, smell me, and breathe me. The living world that I inhabit and inhabits me is, from the beginning, rhizomatic empathy; it is a mesh of bodies in which each being is entangled with me, affecting my behaviors, emotions, and perceptions. Environmental empathy, then, is not only about sensing non-human beings, but also about an inter-empathy of many beings mingling in their life trajectories, affecting each other in an ecology of inter-sensibilities where each being communicates its pain, anger, anguish, fears, and joys.

It is worth considering whether language is much more than the language of human speech. There is also a common language, a vehicle by which all beings in the world communicate with each other. Merleau-Ponty himself (1957) taught how human language cannot be separated from the other beings of the earth. Without knowing it, the feelings of the place are being received by the body itself, which responds to the emotional changes of the affective environment. Language, more than an essence specific to our species, is the result of encounters in the inhabited sensory world. Our empathic bodies vibrate with the animated landscape in such a way that we are affected by the moods of the places we are in. When we feel the "energy" of a place, when we say that a space has a beautiful energy, we are expressing in speech a sense of hospitality felt corporeally because our resonant bodies echo the warmth of the place, of the song of the territory where we are.

In his wonderful book *The Spell of the Sensuous*, David Abram (1996) continues the Merleupontian proposal to argue that we must abandon the notion that language is simply a code we use to represent things and events in the perceived world, as well as the anthropocentric belief that language is an exclusively human attribute. According to Abram, language "originates in our sensuous receptivity to the sounds and shapes of the natural environment" (p. 76). In his beautiful words, language "can never be definitively separated from the evident expressiveness of bird song, or the evocative howl of a wolf late at night, the chorus of frogs gurgling in unison at the edge of a pond, the snarl of a wildcat as it springs upon its prey, or the distant honking of Canadian geese veeing south for the winter" (p. 80). Abram, in line with José Luis Pardo (1991), suggests that there is a common language, a *language of the earth* that is also our own and extends to all expressive bodies. Thus our own language does not isolate us, nor does it put us in a privileged position at the top of the pyramid of beings on the living planet. On the contrary, it "inscribes us more fully in its chattering, whispering, soundful depths" (Abram, 1996, p. 80).

The words we use to communicate with each other ride on the surface of a deep common language—continues Abram—a language that unconsciously mimics and tunes into the other beings in the world in a shared register. If, as phenomenology has assiduously shown, for our sensitive body there is no phenomenon that is not active, that does not warrant the participation of our senses, that does not call us, that is not a vector that reaches, influences, and involves us, then we can assure that in the most intimate register of our sensitive experience we are, as this author says, resonating before the movement of the air, the leaves of the trees, the dance of the firefly, and in general, alive in an expressive landscape that listens and speaks to us. From the outset, our discourse or speech is affected by many gestures, sounds, and rhythms which belong to an animated landscape branching in our language. We render in language what we learn from the language of the earth, the voice of the birds, the sound of the water, and the roar of the wild beasts. 'We are beings incarnated by a polyphony of voices from our Mother Earth, an emergence of the songs of all the beings that inhabit with us, as expressed in this beautiful poem by Juana Karen Peñate (2002), Ch'ol writer:

The music of the jungle	Isoñil matye'el
comes in my hands,	mi tyilele tyi jk'ä'b,
The rhythm of the day	Jiñi ityip'tyip'ñäyelk'iñil
walks in me […],	Woli tyi xämbal tyi ityojlel […],
and as the fields	che'bache' matye'el
I flow in time,	mi ixän tyi tyamlele k'iñil,
time flows in my voice.	tyamlele k'iñil woli tyi ñumel
	yik'oty ty'añ.'

The most recent research on the origin of human language has borne out this phenomenological and spiritual certainty of the peoples of the earth, assuring that articulate phonetic speech probably arose by imitating the noises of nature, and in particular, birdsong. Humans and birds have been found to share great similarities, such as a mirror neuron system—related to oral learning abilities—(Jarvis, 2004), as well as a homologous gene—the FOXP2 gene (Teramitsu et al., 2004). These anatomical and genetic coincidences explain the striking similarities in innate verbal abilities, learning processes and, in general, oral communication patterns (Pepperberg, 2011). The above is but one example that shows that evolutionary lineages extend to seemingly distant beings, and the inhabitation of places in conjunction with organic entities, daughters of the earth, has provided the deep structure of what we now call human language.

Therefore it is possible to maintain, along with Abram (1996), that human languages are shaped not just by human community but also by expressions of the animate earth, in which we find not only animals but other natural modes that provide clues to a common primitive language. Despite the different languages, reflected in the difference between the bleating of the sheep, the squawking of the goose, the mooing of the cow, the whistling of the wind, the current of the river, or the articulated language of women and men, all modes or expressions of life share a common language. Through it, all act as effectors and perceivers, capable of communicating and modifying their behavior in response to a given signal, forming a single semiotic network that extends across the fabric of life.

The aesthetics of life is a field of affects and relationships between sentient beings that communicate with each other. In the words of Mandoki (2013), it is a semiosphere where the different *umwelt* interconnect through networks of signification. In the vital warp, messages and information flow and stimulate the sensibility of others, weaving all bodies in processes of action-perception. It is a network of sensitivities, of communication, through which some bodies craft a message and a sign to link to and interact with a receiver (Mandoki, 2013). This language of nature is not written in mathematical language as Galileo thought, but rather it is a language of sensibilities, aesthetics, affections, empathies, and intuitions: it is an *environmental affectivity* in which the paths of some bodies affect others by being sentient beings able to react to the presence of the other. Life is sensitivity through and through; it is communication through the language of sensitivity, perhaps the mysterious and enigmatic code of the language of the earth that allows us to inhabit it. From the rock that inscribes on its own body the mark left by water, or the molecule that changes its structure by the encounter with another molecule, to the hummingbird that changes its flight before the reflectance of the flower, or human beings that react to the messages of the weather, the predator, or the food, we all are, without exception, part of the *multiplicity* of sensitive life in which we live because we can feel and communicate because we are sentient beings.

We must therefore contest the notion that language is an exclusively human property, that we are the only talking animal. As Abram says, there is no vital mode devoid of expressive capacity. In the fabric of the semiotic network any sound can be a voice, any color an invitation, and any movement a gesture. That we are not the direct recipients of the message or that most gestures escape us does not mean that the various modes of the earth do not speak out, do not communicate in their own language. All of us interacting, dancing in the thicket of encounters, are exchanging signs, meanings, and signifiers. And in this reciprocity of dialogues it is necessary to understand that the organic entities of the earth are not only capable of speaking to us, of whispering to us, but also of listening to us, of connecting with our actions, words, and emotions. The animate world empathizes with us, it reacts affectively to our presence, because by definition it is sensitive to human actions and spoken words. This is the basis of environmental knowledge, which, as we will see next, consists of knowing how to read, interpret, perceive, and understand the messages and guidance of a speaking earth where meaning takes place and spreads expansively through the rhizome of life.

3

Affective Environmental Knowledge: The Ethics of Contact

The enactive approach of neurocognition was the basis to affirm that cognition is, above all, a process of interweaving between the affective states of our body and the affective states of the inhabited places, and to say that constant interaction with the world makes the territories' affections merge with the possibilities of our corporeal expressions. We contended therefore that cognition always implies sensibility, but not only the sensibility of the one who knows; it also involves the affections of the body-territories. Well, we believe that this argumentation on affective cognition can provide a suggestive perspective for understanding the "environmental knowledge" (Leff, 2002) created over millennia by rural peoples as they intertwined with their territories of life.

We shall understand environmental knowledge based on the definition of "environment" we have followed so far: a tangle of intertwining paths or threads between plants, animals, microorganisms, stones, and countless expressions of life, all accompanying each other through their actions and movements, creating the necessary organization so that all are present at different times, speeds, and scales. Environmental knowledge is then the pragmatic understanding of the rhizome of life, knowledge that learns to inhabit the interweaving between the different becomings of the universe's beings, but which manifest in specific aesthetic forms and concrete territories.

Thus defined, environmental knowledge is the knowledge of the inhabiting-knowing. As we have insisted, this knowledge is made possible by corporeal capacities, by the abilities of our composition as empathic and sensitive beings. Environmental knowledge, then, is knowledge from the body and by the body. This knowledge can be grasped, thanks to the understanding that we are living, embodied beings that learn through affections, emotions, moods, perceptions, and feelings through which each experience is imbued with meaning, together with other capacities such as rationalization and symbolization (León, 2017). This knowledge, however, is not sensitive to all the elements and bodies that are encountering each other and moving. Instead it is practical knowledge, knowledge for action, where the body selects the components of the interweaving trajectories based on intention and the pragmatic objectives of everyday life.

We have chosen the environmental knowledge of indigenous peoples, peasants, fishers, and shepherds to ground this somewhat abstract discussion, but also to show that environmental knowledge—which is the knowledge of inhabiting—is not just the knowledge that we need to re-inhabit an occupied land in the present and the future, but knowledge that is part of the collective memory of peoples around the world. This is sensitive knowledge built by the geography of contact with other bodies. While in the collective history this knowledge has created the necessary conditions to persist, it is also erratic knowledge that has often caused relationships to break down, including the extinction of some beings. We do not wish to idealize the world's rural peoples. It is healthy to see them as made up of affective charges inherent to the human condition such as hatred, thirst for revenge, greed, ego, or attachment to power.

Even so, we believe that peoples' environmental knowledge is proof of what the body has "been able to do" over centuries, an environmental ethics that is productive instead of contemplative, linked to family and community reproduction. It is not a no-touch ethics, like a display window one must stay away from. It is not the ethics of modern conservation, where we live in urban spaces in which everything we do not see is destroyed, while we advocate for the preservation of untouched areas for aesthetic enjoyment. The ethics we are talking about is the ethics of involvement, interpenetration, contact, movement, pragmatic action, and for this there is nothing like the vernacular knowledge which, as we want to propose, is the epistemo-aesthetic foundation of an ethics that recovers the direct contact with the inhabiting-in-the-world.

Following the phenomenological tradition, we will present some characteristics of vernacular peoples' environmental knowledge to continue outlining our proposal for an environmental ethics based on contact.

Knowing by Living, Knowing by Being

Environmental knowledge is art: an art that is acquired by living. It awakens in a territory that is discovered by walking it, feeling it, touching it, eating it, crying it, singing it, smelling it, and listening to it. It is situated knowledge built through involvement with other beings, human and non-human, in a concrete ecological space. Rural peoples around the world know what they know, comprehend what they comprehend and do what they do, thanks to the collective experience occurring in a specific context. This knowledge is the result of active, affective participation with the place and from the place, where the circumstances and biocultural conditions of each territory are fundamental for knowing what is known.

For agricultural, fishing, nomadic pastoral, and hunter-gatherer communities, it is impossible to conceive of knowledge divorced from context, knowledge from "nowhere," since their knowledge cannot be separated from a physical environment and a social and cultural context that is always situated. The nature of this knowledge depends on the interaction of the dwellers with the concrete ecological spaces; it emerges in continuous interweaving with the inhabited place; and in this sense, it cannot be understood apart from the shared concrete ecosystems and cultural horizons. Rather than something that is possessed, it is a dialogue between diverse creatures, humans included, whose paths intertwine in daily life, creating a joint history in which places and communities find themselves mutually folding.

Multiple generations have been developing and preserving technical traditions in long-lasting processes. That is why vernacular wisdom, in the words of Rodolfo Kusch (1976), encompasses the great number of ways of being in the territory; it is a common, intergenerational history of being. It refers to a whole body of knowledge that brings together multiple "sojourns" of grandmothers and grandfathers who shared their know-how with generations of successors. Of course, the common knowledge that is woven together in this way is not free from improvement and refinement, nor is it free from loss and forgetting. It is instead a dynamic history that, generation after generation, has been able to preserve knowledge in the peoples' collective heritage, thanks to practical use and daily experience.

Protection and Maintenance of Vernacular Knowledge

As Alfred Schütz explained, environmental knowledge has a social origin in most cases. Peasant families, for example, do not know how to make terraces, ridges, agroforestry systems, or cornfields. Instead these technical methods are the result of a process of collective reflection derived from the ancestral practice of trial and error. Thus, when a farmer faces a problem, they bring with them a body of knowledge accumulated in the long generational chain of their ancestors which has been inscribed in the social body of knowledge. Paraphrasing Schütz and Luckmann (2003), this knowledge saves each farmer the need to acquire on their own "better" solutions to a problem for which the group has already provided an effective solution. This way, for example, the farmer can draw on the accumulated experience of their grandparents, who for centuries knew how to select and obtain local seed varieties and use them to experiment with different farming methods. The farmer can rely on the inherited ingenuity of traditional Agri-Culture systems for water conservation and intercropping; the integration between locally adapted animals and plants; the biodiversity that often characterizes peasant plots and crops to protect against pests and diseases, provide food for the family and animals, and serve as fertilizer, medicine, or tool (Rosset and Altieri, 2017).

There is a recurring element in environmental knowledge, thanks to which a technical tradition can be maintained. This way, one can act as one has learned from parents, grandparents, and communities. In essence no new solutions are necessary for most problems. If nothing changes substantially, there is no reason to vary the planting season, modify intercropping, or alter activities that are usually done according to the lunar cycles. This routinized dimension of environmental knowledge, this "know-how," makes it possible to repeat past practices. This does not mean that in the social transfer of knowledge between people there is no improvement to the solution to a problem, depending on the characteristics and ecological possibilities of the plot of land. No two orchards will ever be identical. In fact, there will be as many garden models as there are peasant families, and this is partly explained by the fact that knowledge is not only kept alive in the most intimate part of the collective experience, but there is also a dimension of the peasant's individual knowledge which is the product of their unique creativity and private experience.

This biographical nature of the body of knowledge, as Schütz would say, consists of knowledge derived from previous experience that varies from person to person. These learnings are the result of a problem to which a practical solution has been given. From the right technique to drop the hoe on the soil, the appropriate relationship between the temperature of the patient and the temperature of the plant, the right time to cut the wood, to more subtle knowledge such as predicting the time of rain, the direction of the winds, the temperature of the fire at the time of burning, or understanding the behavior of insects in the crop, is largely knowledge that rests on the personal discovery of a world grasped by living in it, and which will serve as a reference for moving meaningfully in the territory. For all novice farmers, there will be one problematic aspect of daily life that they will have to face for the first time—roping a calf, correctly plucking the fruit from the plant, storing the harvested corn, stabling the horse—which will be performed automatically once overcome. This body of knowledge—again following Schütz—will serve as the basis for solving everyday problems. It will manifest henceforth as routine behaviors that do not require attention and the farmer will not be able to reasonably explain "how," "where," or "why" it was necessary, desirable or possible to learn them.

Nevertheless, it is necessary to repeat that the private dimension of peasant knowledge occupies a small space within the body of knowledge. Most knowledge is the result of interaction in a social context, and therefore we cannot separate any individual knowledge from the collective sphere in which these populations live.

As we have drawn from Ingold's (2000) analysis, the child learns the skills of their community guided by more experienced people—often from the same family niche: parents, grandparents, older siblings, aunts, uncles, and cousins—who do not provide a code of steps specifying the action to take. Instead the child learns by attending to each action. This is how the novice hunter trains by joining more experienced hunters who instruct them on what to look for: ethereal clues such as tracks, footprints or the scent left by an animal, or specific sounds that would otherwise be overlooked. By hunting, the child receives guidance for developing perceptual skills to grasp the properties of the forest and learn to identify the key signs for finding the prey (Ingold, 2001). And it is not just in hunting. Many other vernacular skills are preserved, generation after generation, as a result of a process of "education of attention," to use Ingold's terminology. A good example is beginner knitters, who learn by watching their mothers knit, carefully observing their mother's needle handling skills, her dexterity in handling the ball and skein of wool, following hand form and correct needle threading technique, and emulating the type of stitches, knotting, and tightening of the yarn.

Knowing by living and knowing by being is a practical "know-how" acquired through imitation and observation (Ingold, 1990). The learner learns by "doing," by being in contact with the environmental components in pragmatic contexts. This way, each generation develops its own skills under the guidance of more experienced people. Environmental knowledge, such as herbal medicine, planting systems, hunting and fishing techniques, food storage, or the construction of houses with locally available organic materials, is maintained over time, thanks to a history of relationships between experienced peasants and apprentices who are instructed, as Ingold (2008, p. 21) argues, "by being exposed to a situation in which, by facing different tasks, they are shown what to do and what to watch out for under the tutelage of more experienced hands" (Ingold, 2008, p. 21). What this anthropologist wants to emphasize is that knowledge is not passed on like genes between parents and children. Knowledge survives because each successive generation can experience firsthand how to deal with some aspect of daily life, in a similar way to their immediate predecessors.

We must also remember that environmental knowledge takes place in a linguistic environment. When a baby is born in an environment where agriculture is practiced and domestic animals are raised, or where hunting or fishing is common, or where herbal medicine is practiced, their individual situation will be socially and culturally bound from the start. The child will be inhabiting the language—as Heidegger taught—and therefore language will determine their experience in the place where they grow up. Language will provide them with a sense of the world given by the culture they are immersed in. To a large extent, their experiences will be shaped by the language they inhabit, which, as Abram (1996) asserts, is deeply interwoven and attuned to the depth of the valleys, the folds of the mountains, the winding of the rivers and, in general, to the topography of the local landscape.

In fact, no vernacular language can be fully understood in isolation from the ecological features of the territory. Each language, with its own uniqueness, has toponymies, ways of naming and classifying plants, animals, and other components of Mother Earth, which are inseparable from the ecological organization of the surrounding landscape. Even each sound of the oral language—again following Abram—its rhythms, tones and inflections, its accents, metaphors, and tropes, is attuned to the scale, the roughness, the altitude, the climate, the vitality, and the contours of the territory. Therefore, environmental knowledge cannot be divorced from either the language or the specific natural contexts in which peoples live. It acquires meaning in specific ecosystems, such as a particular desert, a certain altitude, a variety of grassland or a coastal area with a particular microclimate, which are brought to the experience of the people through a language enriched by the biological diversity of a living territory.

We can therefore be sure that it is through a history of biocultural relations between people who inhabit a specific space that the great wealth of environmental knowledge has been able to reach our days. However, maintaining the basic elements of knowledge, as Schütz states, depends on two fundamental factors. The *first* is that the cultural and social structure be preserved in its essentials. If abrupt change occurs, as happens with urbanizing, defarming, and homogenizing education, the introduction of decontextualized knowledge, the adoption of the values of economic rationality and productivism, or, in general, the dichotomies of the dominant ontology, certain elements of the chain of knowledge—and even complete areas of it—may be lost. The *second* assumption for maintaining knowledge and skills is that the knowledge remains useful for solving practical problems. When a natural context changes, for example, as an effect of climate change, environmental degradation, or local extinction of species, the technical solution which had been preserved even for centuries may be lost. Of course, a changing environment can give rise to the creation of new knowledge, but there is no doubt that when an environmental setting is radically transformed there is no reason to keep protecting knowledge that is no longer useful. Likewise, as development erodes biotic diversity, language wealth is eroded in unison. If there is less and less fauna, if the birds that used to come to sing and give signals have fled due to the destruction of their natural habitats, the vernacular languages are impoverished, and the knowledge associated with the immediate surroundings is irretrievably lost.

In the same way, technological changes can lead to knowledge being forgotten. Tractorization, for example, brought with it the loss of the ox plow, just as the use of antibiotics or chemically synthesized pesticides led to the loss of indigenous veterinary knowledge, or the introduction of hybrid seeds has led to the abandonment of knowledge associated with native and creole seeds. There is also specialized knowledge that can erode when the community no longer perceives it as useful. The decline of knowledge associated with magic, shamanism, and spiritual medicine with plants of power are cases that illustrate how knowledge specific to certain roles can be lost to scientific rationalization and intergenerational change when a specialized type of knowledge no longer finds generational succession.

Creativity Specific to a Place

Vernacular knowledge is not simply a matter of preserving what has been borrowed from the past. If knowledge is alive, it is because it can be changed, transformed, and manipulated; because it is possible to make it say what it does not say, to jolt it, and use it to think the unthinkable. Peoples are not passive agents who merely receive information from their predecessors. They are active actors with permanent agency who experiment, innovate with curiosity, and react to the environmental and cultural changes that are part of everyday life.

It is true that knowledge has a repetitive dimension. If essentially nothing changes, the process as a "whole" can remain unchangeable. Even so, according to Trinidad Alemán (2016), conditions always have a degree of variability. There are contingent events, such as changes in rainfall periods, longer droughts, drastic disturbances such as hurricanes, fires or earthquakes, or the arrival of a new pest or animal disease, which make it necessary to constantly review practices and experiment according to the available body of knowledge. Peasants, sometimes motivated by these urgent needs but sometimes simply out of curiosity, try either an unknown species or variety, or a known seed from other regions; sometimes they modify the plot layout, change the sowing dates, vary the associations, or apply a new treatment to a sick animal. The probability of success increases to the extent that different alternatives are tested to overcome a contingency. Based on the results, peasants select the best species, varieties or remedies, or they continue to look for other options if the effects are not as expected (Alemán, 2016).

Peasant ingenuity is largely responsible for genetic diversity. It is often said that peasants today safeguard nearly two million cultivated plant varieties, five thousand domesticated crops, and breed forty animal species (ETC Group, 2009). This is because diversity is the basis of peasant knowledge. Thanks to the multiple possibilities that can be followed, the peasantry chooses one option or another, depending on their expectations and predictions, to get everything that the family or community deems sufficient for living. Creativity for finding and implementing new solutions also depends on the ecological opportunities offered by the inhabited place, the individual skills acquired or socially learned, the socially constructed body of knowledge and, as Chayanov (1974) would say, the available labor force in the household unit, and the balance between hard work and usefulness.

When a peasant finds a solution to a common problem, it is likely—depending on the social context of each space—that the new practice, the new use of a known component, the new element within the agroecosystem, or the new tool, will be disseminated in the immediate environment. This may have been the origin of anonymous but widespread practices in various parts of the world, such as contour lines and the A-frame, using flowers to attract biotic pollinators, incorporating biomass, different composting techniques, live barriers, mulching, crop rotation, bioferments, biols and foliar fertilizers, and cereal-legume intercropping. Here and there, different peasants in different latitudes and at different times found similar solutions that gradually became part of the collective heritage.

Of course, conditions continue to change—even more so in times of climate change—which is why peasants continue to test, experiment, select, adapt, and discard options. When one of these experimenters successfully tests a solution to a problem shared with their neighbors, the practice of emulation and learning by example can begin to operate. The notion of similarity, as Jean Robert and Majid Rahnema (2015) mention, is the basis for vernacular knowledge that functions through consonance, sympathy, and empathy. When someone rediscovers forgotten knowledge, or brings new knowledge to the world of life, they can reach other people, thanks to the wealth of relationships: perhaps the greatest of the wealth of peoples. We are referring to the wealth of the personal, face-to-face relationship, which makes it possible to share what we have learned, which mobilizes mutual help and sets reciprocity in motion. One of the founding, reproductive gestures of environmental knowledge is its dialogic character; that is, knowledge that given its flexible, subtle, and mentally intensive nature is enriched during the conversational process. It is the dialogue between "intercessors" (Deleuze, 1985)—neighbors, friends, relatives and, in general, exchanges between people living in similar conditions—which enables creating the art of environmental knowledge.

Perhaps not enough emphasis has been placed on friendship as an essential feature of the phenomenology of this type of knowledge. Even if there is a relatively private aspect to the creation of vernacular knowledge, as we have seen, it is never built in isolation. The phenomenon of environmental knowledge can arise from friendships between people living in the same place or between strangers who encounter each other. It is a fertile ground where knowledge can flourish. Friendship's intrinsic gratitude, the pleasure of sharing and reflecting collectively, is the mortar to assemble this knowledge. Hence the importance of networked communal designs (Escobar, 2016) to rekindle the web of human relationships, recover the ability to create contemporary knowledge, regenerate solidarity and cooperation, rediscover concrete solutions to common problems, unleash dormant creativity, and stimulate the power to act and create autonomy.

Aesthetics of Vernacular Knowledge

There is no doubt that the knowledge associated with traditional systems of cultivation, medicine, textiles, vernacular mining, fishing, hunting, or animal husbandry has accumulated the experience of women and men for centuries as they interact with specific environments. Much of this knowledge has been built through experimentation, research, and the age-old formula of trial and error. As we have analyzed, this knowledge has an inductive character through which individual experiences have evolved into general principles and specific practices. Of course, this knowledge is embedded in stories, rituals, origin myths, and it is amalgamated with the communities' religious experiences.

Even so, we believe that the phenomenology of vernacular knowledge also responds to *aesthetics*. In addition to its meaning related to beauty, aesthetics, understood as *aisthesis*, covers the intensity of sensory perceptions and the knowledge derived from feeling, the affective and the sentient.[1] We cannot understand the manifestation of this kind of knowledge unless we pay close attention to the aesthetic and perceptual criteria that governs, for example, traditional agricultural systems. It is interesting that agroecological peasants do not value a fellow peasant's plot in terms of its productivity, efficiency, yield, and all the classic indicators of agronomy and its economistic rationality. Instead of saying, "that farm has great yields," they praise it through an aesthetic judgment: "that farm is beautiful."

As we have been thinking about this, the concept of *proportionality* that Ivan Illich (1997) borrowed from Leopold Kohr has been instructive. For Illich, the sense of beauty is related to proportion. As we have discussed, the paths and webs are not disorganized. They are not random encounters but follow self-organized aesthetic patterns through which we find the symmetries, proportions, balances, and harmonies that we judge beautiful in the warp of life. What Illich finds interesting in Kohr's thinking is the consideration of what is appropriate in a proportion, the sense of what is right for a place, the right relationship between a system's components. The sense of "the right measure," "the harmony that shines out of the proper proportions."[2]

Our point is that the phenomenology of environmental knowledge, as in traditional agriculture, responds precisely to this vernacular sense: the acute perception of proportions, of balances, of the configuration of what is considered good, as well as the sense of what is disproportionate. One look at the tropical agroecological gardens is enough to appreciate the aesthetic sense of well-diversified farms, the floral arrangements that decorate the landscape, the colorful native seeds, or the birdlife that visits the plot to create a peaceful acoustic environment. These designs are made by peasant gardeners who are embedded in the proportionality perceived by their own senses—the visual impressions, but also the tastes, sounds, and smells.

The phenomenology of Agri-Cultural designs does not respond to a preset plan that must be followed to the letter. It takes place amid the environment's ever-changing circumstances, where peasants improvise, guided by the criterion of proportion, the right measure, and the harmony that must not be altered. Proportionality is a well-incarnated sense, embodied in vernacular knowledge, which offers the confidence that something is going well when it *looks good*, when it *sounds good*, when it *smells good*, and when it *tastes good*. Designing environments for life, as Ingold (2012) would say, is not about adapting to a given place in advance, but about *making* a place for oneself. And there is no better guide for this than the senses, sensibility, and affective order. For millennia, peoples have been guided by a criterion that is rather lost in our times: the good sense of the right relationships between the parts of a system, and the association between beauty and the harmony of proportions.[3]

This good sense, of course, comes from the *wisdom of the inhabited place*. Somehow farmers, fishermen, hunters, and nomadic shepherds have learned through a hermeneutics of the landscape, understanding the aesthetic arrangements that occur without human intervention. They have cultivated their knowledge by forging biomimicry while dwelling in their territories of life. The sense of proportionality has emerged by interpreting the set of aspects present in the ecosystem, which gain significance during the design of environments created for habitation. The aesthetic potential of the place will provide the background for understanding the interactions that must be known and will offer opportunities for good hermeneuticists and aesthetes to be guided by the ecosystem's stimuli they become sensitive to.

The phenomenological tradition has insisted that perception is not a matter of receiving information. It entails *interpretation*, which changes according to the context people are immersed in (Merleu-Ponty, 1957). Thus we choose which aspects of the ecosystem are significant and which are not, so that we can respond appropriately according to the intention and objectives of the specific action. Perception is bound by need, so it is not necessary to be attentive to all types of details occurring at any given time. Interpretation depends on the type of situations occurring at the local level and on the intended action (Clark, 1999). Thus, the unfathomable world of perception becomes partial, and attention is focused, in specific proportions, on the appropriate correlation of the components of the place.

This restricted interpretation of equilibria, this hermeneutics of *multiplicities*, involves environmental empathy as we have been describing it. This empathy becomes an act once we pay attention to the correct relationship in a system that makes it possible for the bee to pollinate the flower, the right proportion in which the ants relate to the beetles in a coffee plantation, or the aesthetic patterns of distribution of various insects in the crop. To understand these appropriate relationships that come from the wisdom of ecosystemic self-organization, we need empathic interpretation: that which calls to connect, to be amazed, to be affected, to be involved bodily, and to select the wisdom of encounters that occur in the place, according to the purposes and goals of everyday life. This is undoubtedly sensitive knowledge in which we learn to know according to the affective states and the aesthetic compositions of the world in which we dwell.

Affective knowledge means attuning to what is pleasant or unpleasant to the other's body, like learning to connect with the sensibility of plants in terms of their preference or repulsion for certain conditions of light, temperature, humidity, soil nutrients, chemical compounds in the air, wind, gravity, proximity to other plants, insects, or toxins, or being sensitive to the aesthetic bias of animals for certain scents, colors, flavors, and shapes. When interacting with the *wisdom of the place*, peoples sometimes attribute emotions to plants, animals, and mountains. It is well known that the Mesoamerican *milpa* must be spoken or sung to so that it does not become sad. The Mayan Q'eqchí' of Guatemala hang underwear on fruit trees to make them feel ashamed so that they bear fruit again.[4] The farmers in Chiapas, Mexico, where we live, say, "the plant wants water," which is a reaction to what "the plant's want" feels. Likewise, in many cases tsunamis, hurricanes, eruptions, and earthquakes are associated with the anger of Mother Earth. In all these cases, what occurs is a sensitive, affective communication that arises from interpreting non-human entities we can interact with empathically.

It is likely that vernacular knowledge based on aesthetics could well be rooted in a phylogenetic history through which our species has developed certain tastes and pleasures necessary for survival. So we find beauty and value color vibrancy, symmetry, proportion, balance, and harmony, and we find ugliness in other characteristics that warn us of what is inappropriate for our bodily composition. Without realizing it, knowledge, through the intergenerational network of biocultural coevolution, is sustained by certain aesthetic prohibitions and demands by favoring some qualities over others to the extent that we find them pleasant—perhaps because we associate them with safety, convenience, utility, or pleasure—while we find others repulsive—because we consider them disgusting, shameful, ugly, or inappropriate (Mandoki, 2013).

Our tastes and needs—which vary between peoples and cultures—are biased by evolution. We are attentive to all aspects of other bodies that are pleasing to our bodily sensibilities—we like a flavor, a sound, or an aroma. Although environmental knowledge is largely explained by processes of attunement, intonation, and empathic coupling with the wisdom of the place, it is also true that we tend to imitate only what is pleasant to us. In particular, we tend to mimic only aesthetic qualities that are evolutionarily related to vitality and health, such as color intensity, and certain regularities such as chromatic contrast, rhythm, emphasis, and exuberance, while we disdain dispersion, confusion, and pallor of expression (Mandoki, 2013). Peoples usually use this aesthetic bias in their technical elaborations, where spaces are separated by color, shape, or contrast, as in certain polyculture designs in Andean and Mesoamerican peoples, in hydraulic systems such as the *subaks* in Bali, or the oligarchic forest architecture as in some cases in Australia, Sub-Saharan Africa, East and South Asia, Mesoamerica, and the Amazon (Rivera-Núñez, Fargher, and Nigh, 2020).

An important feature of aesthetic knowledge is that we may think beauty lies in the senses of the perceiver. However, from an affective phenomenological perspective, it is the place itself that frames the inhabitant who perceives it. The territory invents the eyes capable of seeing it, the ears capable of hearing it, the skin capable of touching it, the sense of smell capable of savoring its aromas, and the tongue capable of tasting its fruits. As José Luis Pardo (1991) teaches, instead of thinking that the senses signify spaces, and that the make-up of organisms introduces perspectives; instead of believing that the bodily faculties make it possible to discover the beauty of the world, perhaps we could better say that the territory is inscribed in the body as a mark: the inhabitant and their senses are the product, the result of the place's intertwinings. The territory makes the inhabitant.

History is always the story of how people populate spaces and invent their habitats, continues José Luis Pardo, but not the story of how spaces populate people, and how, in the process of populating them, they transform them. To inhabit a place is, at the same time, to be inhabited, to undergo an effect and an affection, a modification in the sensibility, a change in the senses. The task is therefore to think about how the place is inscribed, engraved, tattooed, and imprinted on bodies; to think how territories fold, leave impressions, and wrap themselves around bodies. But according to this author, for there to be a force that inscribes itself, there must be a surface of inscription, a sensitive body that responds. On the one hand, an ecosystem-effector, which acts as an affecting body; on the other, a perceiver-receptor, affected by the action of the affecting body. In reality, there is no one and the other—no subject and object—but a web of bodies among bodies mutually interweaving, folding, and retracting.

Proportional Lives and Sense of Proportion

The attuned sense of proportionality of many of the vernacular peoples we have been talking about, in addition to the aesthetic aspect translated into an intuition of what is appropriate for the place, can also be explained by living in contexts where proportional lifestyles are guided by the principle of sufficiency. For this reason, the production of peasant plots is limited to what they consider sufficient to live on, avoiding the desire to shamelessly maximize productivity. This art of good living conceals a recognition of proportion within the plot; it includes the right balance between sufficiency and amount of work (Van der Ploeg, 2013).

A fundamental point for what we want to argue below is that the vernacular knowledge of rural peoples has a highly specific feature: the direct relationship with the place that somehow explains their finely tuned sense of proportionality. The example offered by Pierre Madelin (2016) is quite illustrative. Let us think of gathering wood, the main source of energy for many of these peoples. According to Madelin, this activity allows populations to be aware of the natural limits of extraction. On the one hand, if too much firewood is extracted, the forest's self-regeneration limits are exceeded. On the other hand, if too much wood is gathered, beyond the amount needed to heat the house or cook, there is an excessive amount of hard labor. Wood gathering helps understand how the sense of proportionality, the right measure, and proportional living operates in vernacular peoples. This is not due to any moral superiority, but because the work and the direct perception of the context from which energy is obtained provides an idea of the effects of over-extraction and an appropriate balance between the workload and the amount of firewood considered sufficient to meet the family's needs.

The above is just an example to show how the perception of proportionality associated with aesthetics, the workload balance, and the sense of sufficiency, as well as the daily interaction in small community environments, explains to a large extent the environmental knowledge based on the being, which contrasts with modern societies that have lost the ability to have a notion of their energy expenditure and the impact of their consumption habits.

We should also point out that the environmental knowledge of indigenous societies, in addition to the beings visible in everyday experience, is associated with other types of worlds inhabited by beings such as naguals, masters of the mountains, master of the caves and hills, spirits of the jungles, or elves: guardians of sacred places which are communicated with through ceremonies, rituals, and offerings. This communication is entrusted to shamanic specialists, who serve as a means to interact, negotiate, and mediate with these beings through trance, plants of power, fire, or dreams. As Abram (1996) recalls, this knowledge is environmental. The entities that the shamans communicate with by expanding their states of consciousness are not beings from "the beyond." They are the same natural entities we contact to converse with them face to face on their own terms.

All these forms of worlds show that the environmental knowledge of indigenous peoples—at any latitude—is not reducible to the logic of modern ontology. Such epistemes are associated with a relational ontology where there is no separation between human and non-human entities (Blaser, 2009). Environmental knowledge is religious, in the original meaning of the word *re-ligare*, or "re-linking," as Xavier Zubiri calls it: a link between peoples and the other spheres of the universe. It is precisely this deep relationship of environmental knowledge with the cosmos and with other bodies we coexist with in other dimensions, which helps to understand the vernacular feeling of rootedness to the place, which requires asking permission to intervene the skin of the earth, and that needs to be always reconnecting with something greater that exceeds us.

This sense of belonging is expressed in ceremonial worship practices, as well as in pragmatic activities. The vernacular environmental knowledge is there, embodied, solving practical and daily problems in the homes of families, but it is inseparable from the spiritual dimension, from the dialogue with other soul entities that also inhabit the territory. Hence, the refined sense of connection with the beautiful, the pleasant, and the harmony of a relationship is inseparable from the link with the great diversity of bodies—visible and not visible—that accompany us in different dimensions.

For the purposes of our discussion, it is important to understand that the environmental knowledge of peoples has been tied for millennia to a relational ontology, an affective onto-aesthesis, in which the boundaries between human and non-human are deeply porous, and in which the sense of belonging to place has deep roots. And this is not due to any higher moral endowment, but to a reason that appears easy to understand: the history of peoples is the history of direct contact with the elements and beings of the world, and the direct relationship with the body itself. For the vernacular peoples, if you feel hungry you must harvest, raise, or hunt food; if you feel cold you must go to the forest to look for firewood; and if you feel thirsty you must go to the river, the well, or harvest rainwater. All these actions are inextricably linked to the cycles and rhythms of the reproduction of life and to the immediacy of one's own body.

For these peoples there is an inseparable relationship between making, ritualizing, and inhabiting: an unbreakable bond in which people have not been separated from what they can do with their own hands in direct contact with other bodies. They have not been expropriated of their ability to provide for themselves, nor have they been deprived of confidence in their own sensible judgment of what is good and right for the place.

The Ethics of Inhabiting-Knowing

We believe that by exploring vernacular knowledge we can understand the link between daily life and maintaining relationships in the territories that provide the elements necessary to live. Through contact—through direct relationship—we have understood, through the centuries, the phenomenon of encounters, paths, and entanglements; we have sensitively known the characteristics of the bodies that meet and affect us, we have clearly understood the mixtures that do not suit the totality of beings that make up the sentient universe that surrounds us, and we have sought the most harmonious relationships. Knowledge about the features of the other bodies we contact daily has helped us understand, in long-term trajectories, what kinds of relationships, knowledge, aesthetics, and actions are required to enable the reproduction of life, and which others may mean the breakdown of territorial relationships.

What we want to insist on, based on the environmental knowledge of the vernacular peoples, is the possibility of an ethics built as a correlate to a type of ontology of life—collective rather than individual—based on contact and active-affections. This ethics speaks to us of cultivating *potentia*, the inner power, the collective capacity to act and to create a politics of life and for life, and an affective power to act in the face of the devastation and war that our species has declared on the world. To cultivate sensitivity, empathy, and the affective loop that enhances action, means cultivating a type of common affectivity in which we teach each other to be touched by the emotions of others, to pay attention to the phenomena of encounters, and to value the sensitive and sentient experience of the otherness that we also are.

It is about paying attention to our intercorporeal constitution and understanding the right action based on our own sensitive experience. We are not talking about actions motivated by rational calculations or habits, or obedience to the normative aspects of society, but about an embodied ethics based on the willingness to be affected by the encounter with the world's beings. We are thinking of a type of behavior that respects the continuity of compositions. Not an ethics that pursues human perfectibility, but a pragmatic and productive ethics that learns to inhabit interrelationships, as countless peoples around the world have done for millennia. An ethics of inhabiting is the ethics of learning to know how to be—and to love—the place, and to know how to reside in the interweaving of becomings.

Ethics based on *environmental affectivity* is not an essentialism. It also means understanding our shadows, our imperfections, and our dark dimension—not just our light—because we are human beings made up also of horrors, of affectivities that destroy us. The relational ontology must therefore be understood in its complexity because "feeling belonging to" does not always derive in ethical actions without contradictions or rifts. The fact that in the aforementioned communities there is continuity between nature and culture does not mean that "harmonious" relations are constantly taking place. They also exhibit questionable acts and relationships uncoupled from the existence of other beings. And on the other hand, we should also stress that though our modern culture sees the world through the lens of its dichotomous episteme, that does not mean that we moderns always and everywhere have a destructive attitude toward animals and plants, and that at every step and feeling we are fully congruent with our inherited ontological splits. Simply put, all cultures must cope with their contradictions, with the fact that they are inhabited by multitudes.

The ethics based on the environmental knowledge of the rural peoples of the world must be understood with its own problems. Life, according to these worldviews, is a holistic whole, not reducible to individual elements. When ancestral populations say that everything has life, and that nothing is inert, in pragmatic terms this means that it is necessary to give continuity to the conditions that make the reproduction of Mother Earth possible, and not to individual entities. This does not mean that one cannot hunt for food—according to community norms and agreements—that animals are not raised for the family and community diet, that fishing is not carried out in accordance with the environmental knowledge of the group, or that one does not have to deal with a pest that eventually affects the crop or kill insect vectors of disease. In pragmatic terms, the ethics of knowing how to inhabit means that human actions do not violate the compositions of the *multiplicities*, but this does not imply respect for the life of each of the members that make up the vital fabric. And this is where this ethics becomes problematic, because it may be incompatible with the values of vegetarianism or veganism, both of which are as respectable in their principles and as valuable in terms of their compassionate action toward the uniqueness and suffering of animals. If environmental knowledge is conceived without empathy for singularity, we can be indifferent to cruel practices toward some bodies and still comply with the principle of respecting the relations of the totality. In fact, misunderstood ethics of this type can give rise to ecofascism and totalitarian criteria of the type, "if what matters is the whole, it would be acceptable to sacrifice some of its members for its sake." It is therefore essential to balance the principle of actions appropriate to the place and ethics toward individual bodies.

Environmental ethics based on environmental knowledge is not universalizable. It does not start with *a priori* knowledge that can be written down and become normative, like Kantian ethics. The environmental ethics of peoples is relative, flexible, contextual, dependent on practical motivations, and there are no categories of good and evil that can be adopted generally. The ethics of inhabiting-knowing are situated and diverse, as are affections and feelings. They are part of an ontological positioning in which one is ethical by virtue of the affective experience derived from the direct contact with the specific bodies among which one lives. This does not mean that it is an ethics that solves all problems in one fell swoop. In the hybrid condition of the peoples of our times there are marks of power, perverse syncretisms between modern and non-modern elements. Often peoples adopt—or have had imposed on them colonially—the worst of modern culture, combined with the worst of their own culture.

The thrilling thing about taking up vernacular knowledge is that it helps nurture a different kind of environmental ethics: to think about the right actions not in terms of habitual response patterns or adherence to rules (Varela, 1992), but in the midst of the complexity, commutations, affective networks, and mundane situations in which our collective life takes place. As Mariana Borja (2018) states, this is the reign of contradiction, of the struggle between opposites, where good and evil, light and shadow coincide. Vernacular ethics is an ethics of uncertainty that demands respect and enshrinement through offerings, rituals of permission, gratitude, and affection for the constant reproduction of life, since human existence depends on the web of life as a whole. This ethics prioritizes the communal good over individual desire, the reproduction of life over material goods, the understanding that knowing how to live requires permanent work for life to continue, and a direct relationship with the territory in order to refine the sense of proportionality, of the right measure, of what is appropriate for the place.

This ethics, rather than owing to contemplative purposes—appreciating the beauty of the landscape, for example—follows the productive, pragmatic criteria of everyday life. It is an ethics of dwelling among bodies, not outside external "nature," but always inside, occurring among becomings. This, of course, is not free of contradictions, such as recognizing relationships before individuality, but the interesting thing about this ethics based on the immediacy of life is that—as Borja continues—it does not seek to establish a moral code of pure goodness, but rather recognizes the contradictions inherent to the human condition; it does not try to deny or overcome them. As we will see in the next chapter, we shall consider an *ethos* that, instead of aspiring to an absolute and pure good, recognizes and cares for the shadows, and explores and renders conscious the contrary energies.

But above all, the appeal of drawing inspiration from vernacular practices that are sustained by contact, interaction, interpenetration, and involvement with the world is their ability to teach that therein lies the origin of the sense of moderation, and the intuition that something is right when one feels good, to the extent that one has learned to empathize and to be happy for the affection in which one is involved. From that feeling comes the knowledge of the right balance between one's own actions and the actions of other bodies, the balance to achieve the right combinations, but also the wisdom by which one knows when an action is disproportioning a relationship, and the way in which it can be brought back to its proper condition. The environmental *ethos* is active. It arises from movement, from active-affection, from the virtuous combination of the beauty and pleasure of being-here. By interacting with the world we learn how to modify the earth favorably to achieve the right measure, a balance between the sense of sufficiency of daily life and the proportions and beauty of the place.

From this understanding we can say that inhabiting-knowing is above all an art that requires attunement, affective intonation. It is the art of achieving a good tone, as in music, through which the action of the body is coupled with the action of the rest of the corporealities. But this art, this harmony, as we have mentioned, depends on the sense of proportion: the aesthetic sense that guides us when something is right and alerts us when it is not. It refers to the proportion confirmed by sensitive perception, by the body itself, by the fundamental sense we count on to orient ourselves and to know how to inhabit the world. Thanks to the sense of proportion, I can tell when something is correct because my senses tell me that there is a certain right proportion between one side and the other, one color and the other, one sound and the other, one taste and the other, and one texture and the other. It is here that we find the key to an inhabiting-knowing that keeps its roots in the sensitive intonation with other bodies. This *ethos* is based on proportionality, on a shared well-being that is built on the basis of a convenient tension between oneself and the cosmos. What then is the right measure? What is the appropriate proportion? The one that makes me feel good, be well; the one that connects me with the beauty of the universe.

But that valuable sense of proportion requires direct contact, for it cannot possibly arise at a distance. Contact means using your hands, touching, being touched, or doing. It means recovering the ability to work in the workshop and on the plot of land, places where the elements necessary for one's use can be manufactured—so that they are durable and repairable, technologically soft but mentally intensive—and spaces where the proportion between the mind's work the hands' work can be recovered, as well as reconquering the capacity for self-provision. It is in these spaces that inhabiting can intertwine with doing and ritualizing (Ospina, 2018), because for contact to be ethical it also requires respect, scruples, a sense of sacredness and spirituality. These are traits necessary to know what is good and right for the ground trodden, the air breathed, the water drank, and the ecosystem inhabited.

These distinctive features make environmental ethics different as we understand it. It is not altruism; it is not conservationism. It is not staying on the sidelines. It is not the ethics of the dualistic separation between nature and culture: humans in the cities, others in the countryside, in "nature." Instead, it is a pragmatic ethics that uses technology, symbolization, sensibility, and knowledge specific to the place. It transforms by tuning itself and maintaining proportions. It relates directly with the sentient beings of the world. It is the ethics of inhabiting among *multiplicities*, among trajectories, always encountering other types of bodies. It is an ethics that bets on a new civilization: a pluriversal civilization based on regenerating community spheres and recovering the sense of proportionality. After all, this ethics is based on knowledge founded on being, which is understood as the support of post-extractivist, post-capitalist, post-industrial, and post-consumer worlds, which move toward bringing the current imbalance of the urban-industrial system back to a proportional condition.

Collapse and Environmental Affectivity

Why start from vernacular environmental knowledge? What about urban dwellers who have lost any possibility of direct contact with the diversity of bodies that populate the world? Is this ethics not a nostalgic, bucolic, and romantic projection, totally removed from the urban reality of most of the world's inhabitants? We should remember that the city occupies a tiny fraction of our brief history on this planet. We need only consider that the history of our species is at least three hundred and fifteen thousand years old, while the first urban civilization dates back only seven thousand years. Although this may seem a lot, the urban population has been a minority during the three thousand one hundred and fifty centuries of human history. The share of urban people exceeded the share of rural inhabitants only a couple of years ago. Even so, if we were to add the peri-urban population with agricultural practices, we could still say that the Earth is still mostly peasant.

However, we must admit that the last few decades have seen marked urbanization. If we did a linear forecast based on this population trend, we could only say that there will be no end to the growth and expansion of the current urban-industrial civilizational model. We could only assure that in the future everything would be bigger: larger population, bigger cities, avenues intersecting each other, taller skyscrapers. In this scenario, it would not make much sense to think of an environmental ethics as we have been discussing it.

Our starting point is different: in history there are not only continuing trends, but also disruptions and radical changes that occur when societies are no longer able to live the way they used to. As has been well documented (Fernández and González, 2014; Taibo, 2016), it is physically impossible to sustain the growth of the current civilizational model indefinitely, since the material and energy that has supported it is running out. We are at the beginning of the end of the fossil fuel era, and it seems there is no alternative that can replace them to sustain this same civilization. There is growing evidence that we are on the verge of drastic change, as the natural conditions that supported the dynamics of accumulation are running out. This may be the key to the collapse of the urban-industrial system that has expanded around the world since the mid-seventeenth century.

We have reached the end of the party of waste and abundance of energy and mineral bodies, in a context of climate change and pollution. We must rethink the future of a society that still sees the city as the goal for all peoples and still believes that we are doomed to an ever more hyper-technological and artificial world.

Environmental thinking, countering the technological optimists, has been appropriating collapse as the basis for thinking about a radical transformation of the environment. In this field of work, many of us argue that the globalized system of production, distribution, and consumption dependent on oil, gas, coal, and mineral extraction, which causes soil degradation, water and atmospheric pollution, as well as climate change, is destined to disappear. We believe that the only viable alternative is relocating economies, downsizing, shifting settlements, and repeasanting. We believe in recovering a simpler, more austere and smaller-scale life, finding new ecological stability while regenerating community spheres, as has been happening in different parts of the world, some of them documented and discussed by us in other works (Giraldo, 2014, 2018; Mier y Terán et al., 2018; Val et al., 2019; Toro, 2021).

This is the backdrop for the environmental ethics discussed in this chapter. It is not an ethics embedded in the urban-industrial logic, but in the affective, sentient, and sensitive revolution of a civilizational transformation. It is about reappropriating environmental knowledge and the knowledge of the body itself, as is happening in the politics of the margin, in centripetal politics, projected from the periphery of cities. This ethics recovers contact with the sentient beings of the world—human and non-human—and puts its trust back in the affections and the good sense of proportionality of environmental knowledge. Of course, for this we must recognize that epistemicide and the erosion of contextualized knowledge are serious effects of modernization and development. Fortunately, there are rich pockets that refuse to die. They exist in the peoples' common heritage, solving everyday problems. We must create mechanisms to reflect on this knowledge, politicize it, revalue it, enrich it, and empower it by revitalizing relational riches to offer autonomy and the power to act from the territory.

Collapse is always the best opportunity for change. And since each civilization carries its own affectivity, we need to think about the kind of affectivity we need to build those other worlds that so many of us are fighting for. This affectivity is mindful of the encounters between the *multiplicity* of bodies that wander in the entanglements that shape us. It knows the specific paths of each place and inhabits among them, thanks to the environmental knowledge that is woven in community spheres. We will have to build this *environmental affectivity*, recognizing that this knowledge still exists and is kept alive in the deep geographies, and that it is urgent to learn from them, to be inspired by them, to build assembling devices. Thus we can gradually reorient desire, transforming language, disrupting the collective imagination, recovering the power to act from our own bodies, and weaving relational riches between close people in bonds of friendship. This is a bet on other multiple, pluriversal civilizations, which strives for a good lifestyle in harmony with the good lifestyles of the world's other sentient beings.

Even so, we cannot afford to dream naively. It is important to accept that it will be difficult to find this kind of *environmental affectivity* if we do not first understand the affectivity that still sustains this collapsing system.

4

Regime of Affectivity: The Order of Disaffection

We have discussed how our existence is a permanent process of embodiment in which we incorporate the multiple affections, sensitivities, and feelings of the space in which we reside. To inhabit a place is not to remain in passive spaces, but to find ourselves in active places that inscribe in us their forces, folds, and energies. We are the traces, impressions, and marks of the environment in which we dwell; we are affective bodies that adopt in a sentient way the stimuli from the territory in which we find ourselves. *Environmental affectivity* is, on the one hand, to affect the place with our actions; while, on the other hand, it is receptivity to be affected in the body by the atmospheres of the place. We are to a great extent—as are the webs and mixtures of the bodies that inhabit us—embodiments of the affections of a shared environmental, social, and cultural territory.

We have addressed how the affectivities of a place favorably affect the body; however, we must also explore the less numinous aspects of the human psyche, our shadows, and the seamier part of our territories of existence. What kind of affections is inscribed in our bodies when we inhabit landscapes where cruelty toward all forms of life is normalized? What are the intensities of cruelty that are incorporated when we become accustomed to being in spaces where the webs of life are reduced to commodities? We are not only affected by the positive influences of the atmospheres that surround us; we are also affected by the hatred, selfishness, greed, fear, revenge, and profound cruelty that characterize a large part of contemporary society.[1] In line with Rita Segato (2018) we assert that this type of embodied affectivity arises when the constant repetition of violence causes us to become accustomed to it, and the low levels of empathy required for the normal development of the predatory enterprise are established. Once cruelty becomes not the rare but the norm, not the exception but the rule, our bodies inevitably become desensitized, anesthetized to the suffering of others. Gradually we can no longer feel the pain of the mountain as pain, the cry of the earth as a cry, or the cry of the forest as a cry.

We mentioned that empathy is a possibility, a biological potential, which may or may not be expressed depending on the environmental conditions people live in every day. If we live in spaces where the norm is devastation and the reiteration of cruelty toward all forms of life, it is understandable that the deep lack of empathy and the cycles of disaffection that prevail in our time become installed in our bodies. The environments of development and progress favor psychopathies associated with the inability to feel the pain of others. As we become accustomed to living in their intense desensitizing radiations, we lose the biological ability to feel the emotion of others, transforming everything else into an inert object. The erosion of empathy is a collective disease, a common state of mind, a psychic pathology that enables the dehumanization of humanity and the denaturing of nature, two features of modern fascism.

The affective state of our civilization resembles the psychic state of the pervert: incapable of stopping the narcissistic desire that forces them to disregard everyone, since the only thing that matters to them is their own satisfaction and the fulfillment of their obsessions. We are collectives which, having eroded the empathy of its members, suffer from high thresholds of insensitivity that enable the destructive impulse associated with a great difficulty to establish bonds and to feel what the other feels. Impervious to the sensibility of *multiplicities*, we can do whatever we want, regardless of whether this desire prevents the conditions for life to continue being life, and for bodies to continue living among other bodies. The loss of empathy explains in large part why people commit such cruel acts without compassion or remorse. We have been welcoming in our own bodies the destructive traces, the thanatic forces we are all victims of when we live in spaces where wickedness has become the norm, and where the mutilation of Mother Earth is trivialized and justified so that the desire for progress can be installed over the wounded skin of the territories.

Environmental affectivity must examine how our empathy becomes disconnected, how common people become accomplices of devastation, and how a lack of empathy is the ideal channel to enable the sensitive order necessary for dividing *multiplicities* by establishing the predatory project.

Ecology of the Ominous

We will pause a bit to go deeper into how the affective order of a human group operates. To do this we must begin by considering that the Spanish word *sentir* (feel) and what is *sentido* (felt) by our "sensibility" comes from the Latin *sentire*, linked to the Indo-European root *sent* whose meaning is to guide or give direction. Hence, feeling is above all a directionality. It is the direction we give to the specific ways in which we experience life. Sensitivity is the ability to give a particular meaning to the phenomena we encounter, and to give meaning to the sensations and alterations of the organism (León, 2011). Thus, feeling a river as a dwelling, a mountain as a resource, an animal as an object, or a forest as a sibling does not mean that these beings exist in that way, but it is the direction that our feeling has given to the experience.

We began this text by asserting that all forms of rationality imply a type of affection, and that ecocidal reason is not irrational. It is rather a reason that is oriented, guided, and directed by a feeling—*sent*—provided by cultural codes. While we may think that emotions such as joy, sadness, fear, shame, or anger are traits exclusive to our personality, these emotions are also conditioned by the sensitive patterns of our societies. Hence, the feeling-thought that provides the logic for exploitation, objectification, and devastation of vital webs is guided by collective affections, by a sensitive order given by the matrixes of social significance.

There is a kind of insensitivity that explains the cruel acts against the earth, but this must be well understood. In reality it is impossible to be anesthetized as if the nerve plexuses that innervate our skin were blocked. But we can be sure that the collective sensibility can be reoriented, giving a direction to what may or may not be felt. Sensibility is always selective, and this selection is determined by cultural influxes that give a particular meaning to the phenomena we come into contact with. They tinge reality with a specific hue, like a kind of light that illuminates and conditions our way of feeling. For those of us living in cultures that turn the earth into a dispirited object, the erosion of life—instead of arousing discomfort, depression, anger, or melancholy, and mobilizing our actions to stop such barbarism—is met with indifference. The biased sensibility of modernity makes us impassive in the face of ecological ruin and quite susceptible to the stimuli of our individual economic interests.

The selective capacity to distinguish between what is important and what is not functions as an affective regulation, a process of discrimination that responds to what Ciompi (2007) calls *affective economy*. With this concept, the author suggests that the situations that could potentially affect us are unlimited, but this is of course an impossible assumption. If we reacted sensitively to each and every daily event in our world, our emotional energy would inevitably overflow, since each affectation entails considerable investments of energy. Modulating our emotions is crucial for preserving the body's homeostasis. If we allowed ourselves to be affected by all events, it would trigger an emotional collapse. Economizing is a defensive strategy to achieve stability and avoid becoming shipwrecked in the affective sea. Were it not for that affective arrangement, our powers would be subsumed in chaos; we would die trapped by the force of any incitement, outburst of euphoria, anger, or sadness (León, 2017).

We must understand that the affective economy is shaped by a cultural and social referential framework, which provides the "affective rails" common to a specific human group (Ciompi, 2007). These rails regulate the affective economy, providing the route, the scripts, and recurrent responses by which the collective will value, reward, repress, and punish the sensitive experience. Affective rails are a sort of emotional memory that determines how things appear by selecting what is considered important or appreciable, while discarding the trivial and unimportant, thereby avoiding unnecessary energy expenditure (León, 2017).

This idea of affective rails can also be viewed through the lens of *ordo amoris*, "order of love," an Augustinian notion taken up by phenomenologist Max Scheler (2003) to assert that affections are not chaotic and capricious but respond to a certain logic and order. For Scheler, the *ordo amoris* is a hierarchical system that organizes feelings and separates what can be loved from what cannot. For Scheler every society functions by establishing the affective inclinations of its members, organizing acts of love and indifference, giving importance and value to certain kinds of objects and things. This provides the framework of preference for what has value, while at the same time modulating, subtracting, or downplaying what does not. The *ordo amoris* is, in the end, the way of organizing the affective economy of society's members.

The aspect we are interested in highlighting is the power relations woven around the *ordo amoris*, because whoever knows the logic of this system of order has one of the most important keys to dominate society. This is what we refer to as the *regime of affectivity*: a system of power that controls the population's sentient horizons by creating the reference framework that dictates what a collective can feel. The *regime of affectivity* forms the sensitive repertoire that establishes the patterns of sensitivities and insensitivities and directs affective relations in a society. It corresponds to the distribution, selection, and government of the sensitive; it organizes the experience of bodies, establishing the things to which our sensibility is directed, establishing which elements we are allowed to love and which we are allowed to remain anesthetized to, and regulating the distribution of the affective economy and the affective rails of a society. By *regime of affectivity* we refer to a way of exercising power that establishes the sentient flows of the hegemonized, so that their behavior and thoughts follow certain courses of action. This way, people who inhabit a certain emotional network replicate a consented and internalized oppression insofar as a specific form of sensibility is embodied and becomes the map that guides thought, action, and perception.

The *regime of affectivity* orders which perceptual data from the environments are meaningful and which are not, so that people can select the elements that serve the desires, aspirations and obsessions of their cultures. Thus, a *regime of affectivity* prioritizes certain aspects, dictating what is meaningful and what is not. In other words, the *regime of affectivity* organizes the *umwelt* or "surrounding worlds"— in Uexküll's words—of individuals, creating sensitivities according to elements that coincide with the unconscious desires and fantasies of capitalist societies. We have insisted that perception means interpreting the context; people biasedly select the environmental aspects that are important according to the specific action objectives. Well, the *regime of affectivity* of our societies organizes corporeal perception causing a perceptive bias toward technological goods, merchandise, and advertising, while rendering imperceptible the sensitive elements of the earth that are depredated to make possible the excesses of hyper-technological cities.

As Bourdieu (2016) explained, taste is a socially constructed disposition that classifies the elements that cause sensitive pleasure, that arouse admiration and attraction, that charm us and make our emotions vibrate, and that seduce and delight the senses; and at the same time taste offers the perceptive schemes concerning the unpleasant, the repugnant, that which we push away because it is considered the opposite of what causes pleasure. The *regime of affectivity* creates models of embodied dispositions through which people adopt an aesthetic viewpoint that recognizes beauty in urbanizing aspects, in the artifacts of thermo-industrial civilization, instead of seeing ugliness and rejecting the aggression against the configuration of life. This is particularly important in shaping modern ontology. If our species, in the course of its evolutionary history, developed certain aesthetic biases, tastes, and pleasures useful for survival, finding beauty in what is appropriate for our bodily composition, and warning against whatever denies vitality and health, it is worth thinking about the distortion of the aesthetic bias by which we can no longer recognize poison as poison; we stopped perceiving the risk of death and lost the ability to choose what is appropriate for our life based on its aesthetic condition.

Capitalism's *regime of affectivity* has modified our senses. It has made us incapable of seeing the beauty in life, for beauty has moved elsewhere. We can no longer see beauty in darkness: in a dark starry night, in the fireflies blinking at dusk. We have traded it for the illuminated cities, the bright light bulbs that turn night into day. This system of socially constructed tastes has robbed us of our capacity to see, hear, smell, and connect with that beauty. Why does this system make us see beauty in an electronic device rather than in the material it is made of? Why do we feel such excessive affection for objects born from planetary destruction? When our aesthetic bias is modified, and with it the ethical criterion that chooses life and rejects the project of death, we become incapable of recognizing what is good for us, what is appropriate for the place. In an ontological, evolutionary backflip against our phylogenetic history, we begin to find pleasant and to perceptually favor that which denies life.

This *regime of affectivity* that orients cognitive understanding, perceptual significations, and aesthetic preferences largely works because it presupposes people's freedom, in such a way that those who are guided by these affective systems think they are free, even if in reality they follow patterns of affection molded by the cultural representations of modern capitalism. It is not, as Foucault taught, a repressive and prohibitive type of power, but a sensitive order and logic that offers pleasure and desire, and that directs the affective response towards itself, while disaffecting and unmooring the links with others and the earth (Giraldo, 2018). Based on their self-perception of freedom, people end up orienting their affective economy toward themselves, configuring a narcissistic, egoic relationship, so that—as Byung-Chul Han (2016) asserts—most of the libidinal energy is used on oneself, while the rest is distributed and dispersed in increasingly superficial relationships.

One of the most important psychic diseases that this regime propagates, according to Han, is the inability to form deep bonds, instead channeling affective energy toward oneself. On the one hand, this makes people drown in a mania for themselves—the narcissistic relationships of the social networks of cyberspace are the best-known symptom—while on the other hand, it makes them unable to empathize with others and feel belonging to an all-encompassing whole. Deterritorialized people become accomplices and victims of planetary destruction as the *regime of affectivity* offers the framework of what to react sensitively to: consumption of goods, comfort, beauty, capitalization of oneself, while providing the framework of what to be indifferent to: injustice and disrespect for life in all its manifestations. The relations founded by this regime are commercial relations, economic transactions, since each person, severed from their humanity and transformed into an entrepreneur, small business owner or merchant, can only build links based on mercantile relations.

The contemporary *regime of affectivity* that directs desire in the face of scarcity—the lack of what is said we must have—also guides us toward predation. Without knowing it, we are depositaries of a psychic apparatus in which a great deal of violence and cruelty nests. We host thanatic energies that we do not recognize as such, because our sensibilities have shifted to the search for merchandise, success, frivolity, and levity. To paraphrase Giorgio Agamben (2017), this is an order of affections in which one can kill without committing crimes, in which sacred life ceases to be sacred, and in which ecocide becomes an externality, just another cost of the economic process. Our capitalist societies run on affective rails where market forces direct the value systems and shape the tone of our perceptions, affections, senses, aspirations, appreciations, passions, and desires around the consumption of goods, while avoiding the affective paths that favor attachment to the land.

As Felix Guattari (1990) would say, this sensitive system functions through a structure of cuts and branches. It simultaneously cuts the vital networks and creates branches and communication channels with the affective rails of the capitalist world. It is an affective ecology, which deterritorializes people from the place and territorializes them in the networks of the ominous. By means of multiple strategies, the system transforms us into Cartesian subjects, detached from the world. It creates beings isolated from each other and detached from the earth, forming a series of dispersed, self-referential, perverse, and narcissistic subjectivities. It is an ecology of death and violence, of cruelty, which works by stimulating the desire for what denies life—which in everyday life manifests in apparently harmless goods and services—forming through bifurcations, vectors, and rhizomatic growth networks of emotionalities related to the predatory project and incompatible with caring for the conditions that make life possible.

It corresponds to a collective eros and thanatos, to an *ordo amoris* of the *homo economicus*, which incorporates the affective economy into the capitalist economy, channeling sensibilities to the enjoyment of commodities, so that capital can be accumulated by dominating the affective embodiment. The destructive energies woven into the ecologies of the ominous erode empathic capacity, rendering us incapable of empathizing[2] not only with human sentience but with the sentience of ecosystems and non-human life forms, which, as we shall see, are one and the same problem.

Violence against the Earth, Violence among Humans

On November 8, 2004, Mamo Mariano Suarez, one of the most respected authorities of the Arhuaco people of the Santa Marta Sierra Nevada in Colombia, was assassinated by guerrillas of the Revolutionary Armed Forces of Colombia. When Mamo Kuncha Navingumu was asked what he thought about the murder of his companion, and in general about the violence suffered by his community during the Colombian armed conflict, he answered the following:

> In the beginning of creation, us peoples of the Sierra were assigned everything that we must obey, both young men and women, we were given complete rules ... This is how he survived the world and complied with the rules of the ancestral mandate. But then the abuse began. This is what is happening now, what we see now. Little by little everything got sicker, and the more we endured the pain, the stronger it became. When we woke up, the pain persisted. They began to cut down our sacred trees. The younger brother does not know that he too has sacred trees. And by cutting them down indiscriminately, they bleed the world. They think that nature is

asking them to do this harm. Fools! It is the Mother herself they are hurting. How much harm the violent ones do by spilling blood! They snatch the life from everything alive. They do not think of the harm they do to all living beings. They kill following a list without knowing why they do it ... They are increasingly aggressive. The worst thing is that they intimidate us so that we do not say anything to them. And their anger burns them like the stones that burn. That's right. They are digging out the entrails of the earth. They are cutting down the mountains, destroying the vegetation. Not content, they are tearing out the heart. For this reason, diseases are increasing ... We need to heal the disease and make spiritual payments. Only this way can things change, by returning to their origin. Then the violence will cool down. And as soon as everything cools down and is handled with respect, what we see will no longer happen.

(Villafaña, Gil, and Gil, 2009)

We have transcribed this account because, in our opinion, the words of Mamo Navingumu clearly express the profound connection between violence among humans and the war against the earth. His opinion, nestled in the wisdom of the four peoples of the Colombian highlands, is that the origin of violence among humans is violence against Mother Earth. Once the sacred trees are cut down, once the entrails of the earth are pulled out, and "not satisfied, they tear out the heart," it is easy to understand that the life of all living beings, including human beings, ceases to be respected. For Navingumu, violence cannot be conceived in an anthropocentric way; it does not begin and end with the cruelty that we humans inflict on each other, but begins with the disrespect for natural life, which extends and radiates to each being, making everything sick, normalizing the cruelty.

The inseparable relationship between the cruelties and suffering caused to human beings and other living beings can take on obscene dimensions in war. When the co-author of this book was doing *compulsory* military service as a soldier in Colombia, he heard that there was a military course for special forces in which the students had to raise a dog for several weeks. During the training in which the soldiers were perfecting their tactics and combat performance, the dog became an inseparable companion. The animal was fed, cared for, pampered and loved. But the final test came at the end of the course. To be approved, all soldiers were forced to perform a sinister operation: they had to kill their own pet with their hands and eat it! Although this story could never be confirmed, there is an intimate relationship between the cruelty inflicted on other beings and the cruelty we inflict on people in warfare.

Rita Segato's concept of "pedagogies of cruelty" is illustrative for naming this type of infamous action. For Segato (2018, p. 13), there is a type of pedagogies, such as this one, in which people are educated, habituated, and programmed "to transmute the living and its vitality into things." The pedagogies of cruelty teach much more than how to kill: they teach how to murder objectified, desacralized beings. In these schools of cruelty that are the armies of all kinds, one learns to despise life, to naturalize acts of cruelty and acquires the ability to become desensitized to the suffering of others. Having to kill a dog one has affectionate bonds with and eat it is an extreme caricature of that *regime of affectivity* in which one learns to show that one has, as Segato (2018, pp. 47–8) puts it, "thick, calloused, desensitized skin," "that [one] has been able to abolish within oneself the vulnerability that we call 'compassion' and, therefore, that one is capable of committing cruel acts with very low sensitivity to their effects."

One example—particularly emotional for us—that illustrates the intimate association between the Colombian war and violence against animals, is the Mapiripán massacre that occurred between July 15 and 20, 1997. In this criminal action, about one hundred and fifty paramilitaries removed forty-nine people from their homes and took them to the municipal slaughterhouse to mutilate them and slit their throats, in a manner similar to what butchers do with cattle and pigs. The space used to slaughter animals served as an ideal scenario for the armed actors to animalize their victims and thus turn the operation into a replica of the procedures used to slaughter animals.[3] Animalizing helps to dehumanize the victims and suppress empathy with them before annihilating them. According to anthropologist Victoria Uribe (2018), who painstakingly studied nearly fifteen hundred massacres of the Colombian war for more than half a century, there is a common pattern in the collective killings of unarmed people by armies: perpetrators often assign the victim an animal identity in order to degrade them, erase their face, deliberately suspend their humanity, induce indifference and suppress guilt. During massacres, it is common to use the same weapons used by rural butchers to slaughter animals, and frequently, as in animal slaughter, the neck is the most damaged part and the carcasses are turned into meat.

The Colombian case is not unique. It is common in war to represent the enemy as an animal. This cognitive operation is aimed at dismantling their human condition, projecting destructive feelings and making it easier to carry out cruel acts. For example, in the Rwandan genocide the Tutsi were called "cockroaches." In the Jewish holocaust the Jews were called "rats" or "pigs."[4] In contemporary wars in Africa the enemy is identified as an insect (Suárez, 2008). The same occurs in all violence against women, since it is common for the aggressor, upon sexually violating them, to refer to them as "bitches." The objective is always the same: to suppress the humanity of the antagonistic group or the person that will be harmed, to create distance and stereotyped affective meanings, so that the natural feelings of compassion are disengaged and the others appear as objects, making it possible to be cruel without guilt.

Behind these psychic procedures there is a feeling-thought and a *regime of affectivity*: human beings are superior to all other beings and therefore, in order to kill or be cruel, I must first degrade the other to a condition of supposed inferiority. In dualistic representations, this means degrading them for being closer to the earth and further from any idea of humanity. The superior/inferior dichotomy has in fact been the reasoning that has justified the massacres and colonial wars waged far from the metropolis. As Tzvetan Todorov (1987) says, the more distant and strange the victims are, the more you can equate them with animals, the easier it will be to exterminate them without remorse. In the conquest of America, to give just one example, the criteria for defining the "barbarity" of a people, and therefore the legitimacy of dominating them by force of arms, was completely coupled to their relationship with the land. The native communities—at that time called "the naturals"—were closer to nature and farther from civilization. They lived in warm climates, their skin was the color of the earth, they were naked, and in general they had certain features that made them "almost beasts" in the opinion of the conquerors.

It is not only in war that animalizing processes facilitate committing acts of cruelty. Those who study the psychopathic profiles of serial killers have found that 98 percent are animal abusers, which habituates them to feeding their sadistic fantasies and trains them to interrupt empathy to commit murder without remorse (Macdonald, 1963). Animalization as a strategy for dehumanization is more frequent than many realize. Suffice it to say how any of us fall into actions of this type when we offend with animal metaphors by calling the other "dog," "rat," "harpy," " chicken," "pig," "monkey," "donkey," or simply "animal."[5]

Speciesism associated with human cruelty functions as a *regime of affectivity* insofar as it defines a *system of equivalences* whose purpose is to distinguish between what can be affected and what cannot. If the referential framework that guides sensibilities teaches that the less a creature physically resembles a human being, the easier it will be to become insensitive to its suffering, it is absolutely understandable that the cognitive solution is to treat the other as inferior by equating them with an animal, thus removing any qualms to mistreating, torturing, or killing them. Using words intended to animalize a victim to turn them into something "less than human" is entirely linked to the sensitive organization that defines which aspects of the world we can be sensitive to—that which most resembles a human—and which others we can remain disconnected, indifferent, disaffected, or disengaged from—the most distant, the rest: nature.

Thus we can comprehend a non-anthropocentric notion of cruelty, and we can understand that *environmental affectivity* is intricately linked to war and with malice and wickedness among human beings. Ecocide, depredation of the earth, and mistreatment of the world are not separate from homicide, femicide, or genocide, because all "-cides" hide within themselves a disregard for life, indifference to suffering, suppression of empathy, and disconnection with the otherness. Cruelty to any living being, be it a tree, human, river, mountain, reef, or animal, is made up of a repertoire of anesthetics that feed off each other, insofar as the exercise of violence, in the face of any vital expression, only encourages and stimulates destructive energies in a chain against all others. We want to emphasize that there is an entropic growth of destruction, a rhizomatic *regime of affectivity*, whose common pattern consists in making people feel they have nothing in common with the other, and that it is therefore irrational to nurture empathic feelings that prevent their annihilation.

When Mamo Navingumu says—faced with the murder of his companion—that violence is against every living being, in a way he is saying, in harmony with Spinoza, that since we are mode and expression of a greater whole, there is no violence that we can inflict on any being that is not simultaneously violence against the others. Violence against sacred trees or the bowels of the earth is also violence against the entire living fabric. Disrespect for life is irremediably linked to a civilizational course that has become a bad mixture, with increasing pain and suffering. This sick civilizational destiny is compromising the life of all. It is a psychic pathology, because in the evolutionary course all sensitive and aesthetic order wants to seek life, not to violate it. It is a collective illness to insist on taking away power, subtracting life, and pretending to be well adapted to the webs of desire and imaginary ecologies that affirm the project of death. We are like hot stones that burn themselves by privileging an accelerated, frenetic, and hot behavior over cold and paused thought that helps us recognize that all damage is a network, chained to everything.

The war of our times, the war against the world, is governed by a *regime of affectivity* that offers guidance on where to connect feelings and how to perceive what is important, what has value. It is a war that uses a dense, interconnected network of insensitivities, in which each act of cruelty draws its specific character from its relations with the others. The *regime of affectivity* that orients sensibility toward the project of death is an active web of ominous phenomena in which perceptions, sensitive experiences, and the senses themselves are aligned in self-referential affectivities, individualized and separated from the earth, forming a vast ecology of aggression and violence.

Words, Sensitivity, and Place

We have said that language transcends the human; it branches out and merges through the vital webs in a deeper language, the language of the earth. On its surface is inscribed the language of the women and the men of multiple peoples, who have built their collective imagination and environmental knowledge in a linguistic diversity closely associated with the biological diversity of their territories. This biocultural intertwining has been the basis of human habitation on the earth's surface. Indeed, to let the voice of the earth flow, to let the sensibilities of the different creatures be inscribed in human speech is—in the long coevolutionary process—what has allowed our fragile species to inhabit a lively earth. Through successes and mistakes, spaces have been transformed and inhabited in an ecology of words in tune with the polyphony of other beings. In the course of this long journey, symbols, signs, and meanings have populated spaces in a semiotic network where humans and non-humans interpenetrate.

The above is important for understanding the *regimes of affectivity* of our times. It highlights the fact that if we want to reorient our collective sensibilities and direct our feelings in accordance with the modern predatory project, the first and most important thing to do is to strip human discourse of its *earthly language*. It is necessary to do away with the environmental knowledge used by peoples and cultures to name and classify the living beings and components of their ecological spaces in order to incorporate people into universalizable, deterritorialized, and decontextualized discursive chains, and into languages that have been intervened by the syntagms, metaphors, and language games of a world that has become an object-commodity.

Linguist Uwe Poerksen (1995) coined the concept of *plastic words* to show that the problem is not only the loss of the enormous idiomatic richness that populates the planet, but that the radical simplification of language has colonized common sense. A handful of words adopted into the common language have invaded the everyday world, with enormous consequences for everyday perceptions and forms of living. According to Poerksen, the plastic words supplied by the language of science, economics, and administration have interfered with how people speak. They have affected their ways of feeling, their sensibility, and their desires. Phrases invested with authority by the expert discourse of international environmental policies, such as "natural resources," "environmental administration," "aesthetic enjoyment," "environmental services," "natural capital," "environmental management," "water resources," "sustainability," and "sustainable development," among many other similar locutions have offered metaphorical meaning to modern rationales in which the living world is transmuted into available objects. Specialized linguistic categories such as these, loaded with authority, pour down from above to guide sensitivity and daily existence with an anthropocentric code, imperceptibly altering the *language of the earth* that our symbols were based on until recently.

The technical meanings inherent in the separation of human beings and nature, on which science is so comfortably based, have conquered the social meaning distinctive to each people which, in the course of evolutionary history, became connected with a language that exceeds the merely human. According to Poerksen (1995), these are words that replace vernacular words coupled to a specific biocultural context with words that are poor in content but have broad application, reducing a huge field of experience into a single expression. As forms of speech used by experts, they increase the prestige of those who use them, make previous words seem old-fashioned, and, above all, once they displace words that emanated from a particular context, they standardize the world and open up sensitive possibilities for further exploitation.

The impoverishment of language is linked to the impoverishment of natural diversity. When a wetland is filled in for real estate, a watershed is converted into a hydroelectric power plant, a river into a mercury sink, a mountain into a stone mine, a jungle into a monoculture plantation forest, or a biodiverse grassland into an oil field, the language is inevitably diminished, because the living beings displaced by the engine of progress embark on the journey to oblivion with no way to return to the memory of the peoples. As thermo-industrial civilization advances, occupying more and more territories, language is also being emptied of the environmental knowledge that only made sense within biological diversity, becoming fertile ground for the violent, anthropocentric enunciations of capitalist modernity.

On a journey through a city infested by freeways jammed with cars and buses, where glass skyscrapers can be seen amidst commercial titans lit by artificial lights, it makes perfect sense to use language devoid of poetic meaning[6] to name a collection of inert, mechanical, and mute objects. In the landscapes of development, the world has ceased to speak to us, because the natural signs and codes that we once felt through our sensory participation and direct contact with the living earth have been replaced by disenchanted, desacralized artifacts. In our suffocating routines, plastic words help us represent everything non-human as a passive thing, without any meaning beyond existing as a useful resource for the women and men who can buy it, or as any other meaning lacking affective attachment.

In the *regime of affectivity* of our times, plastic words have helped to cut ties with the earth, replacing direct relationship and contact with an abstraction and totalitarianism of meaning, in which the technological domination of the planet is constructed and emotionally embraced through objectifying language. Once the language of the earth is squeezed out of human discourse, once our common tongue is ravaged and violated, we become robbed of the experience that has made us human. As Abram (1996) suggests, when we are incorporated into the abstract, economistic and managerial terminology of modernizing language, we end up distancing ourselves from the voices and gestures of the living landscape and directing all our attention to the artifacts and technologies offered in the marketplace.

Poerksen has helped us understand that the *regime of affectivity* is a regime that produces truth. It is made up of compound enunciations consisting of barely a few words. Through the discourse and narrative weaved by these few words we form conscious and unconscious certainties about the world. In the process of telling ourselves a story that denies the active, animated participation of the earth's beings, at the same time we alter our body and its capacity to feel. Language—as phenomenology and the cognitive sciences of enaction have so meticulously analyzed—is rooted in our perception. It has an immense capacity to influence our sensory experience. We see, hear, smell, taste, and touch as guided by our language, insofar as our linguistic habits predispose us to interpret the world a certain way and not another. Therefore, to define the living world as inert, to deny the reciprocity of the earth, and to enunciate our relationship with other beings as if it were a commercial transaction—consider the expression "environmental services"—is to turn our senses away from the parts of the earth that we also are. In that same act, we become blind, deaf, and insensitive to what inhabits us, while our senses become sensitive to other kinds of goods and objects.

However, it is important to understand that our words, discourses and ways of speaking do not only affect our body, but also the bodies of the bountiful earth. If it is true that the earth empathizes with our languages, that the trees, animals, rivers, and oceans tune into and vibrate with our feelings, then we can also say that our indifferent discourses, our narcissistic verbal conventions, also affect the place we inhabit. In an interview by Federico Valdés (2018, p. 190) to the Mazatec *chjinee* Féliz Ramírez, the effect of speech on the inhabited space became clear:

> The word beautifies, sanctifies. It falls like thunder when spoken, it penetrates the place. Words are fulfilling their mission. When the word is good, it works wonders; when the word is bad, it destroys. I am not sure how much it manages to destroy in the core of Mother Earth and in the air. The word tells us not to speak lightly, for we may say something innocently and not realize the extent of the harm we are causing.

This Mazatec shaman is talking about something well understood by the environmental knowledge of the spiritual specialists of many native peoples: the immense power of the word to slip through the warps of the earth and to affect life and its relational mysteries. As Austin (1990) taught, language has a perlocutionary function that allows us to do something by saying. What is this something we do when we express ourselves with the modern codes inscribed in a violent, militaristic language that denies the vivacity of the beings of the earth? How far will the perlocutionary function of the anthropocentric languages of our misguided modernity go? What we do to the inhabited world with our thoughts, feelings, and words will surely remain inscrutable to our limited scientific methods, but we can verify that, having become prisoners in a language intervened by modern capitalism will to power, we have become deaf to the language of the earth, blinded by the ugliness of destructive construction, insensitive to the poison we eat in our food, and profoundly lacking in empathy by losing the biological ability to feel what others feel.

Understanding what happens in everyday life is inseparable from the linguistic codes, discourses, and stories we use to say what is happening, what things are made of, and what our participation in the world is. This is why the *regime of affectivity* that creates serial subjectivities requires enunciations consistent with the sensibilities that are useful to the regime of accumulation and the system of planetary domination.

The Ecocidal Shadow

The *regime of affectivity* extends like a collective shadow: as Carl Gustav Jung (2002) thought, this shadow harbors the darkest part of society. It hides within itself society's most sinister emotions, its undisclosed desires, its most unpleasant characteristics, which it refuses to admit as its own and therefore banishes them to the most hidden side of the collective unconscious. All those feelings and affections that are rejected and cast into the shadows fuel that dark dimension of contemporary societies; they are expressed in the darkest, most aggressive, and fateful behaviors. We are emotional beings who cause pain, who are cruel to other species and destroy their habitats. The *regime of affectivity*—which decides the elements that can be loved and the elements that we can be indifferent to; which modulates and distributes the emotional economy of human groups—has engendered a sort of mass psychosis. It has made people empathically handicapped and has offered the framework of affective possibilities so that the most fearsome acts of ecocidal barbarism can be inflicted and oceans of suffering can be caused to the entire sensitive network.

Environmental ethics must recognize this sinister side of the human psyche, because the more we repress the shadow and try to hide it, the clearer and crueler it is going to express itself. Like yin and yang, we have on the one hand a numinous, empathetic, and sociable side capable of being sensitive to the world; and on the other hand, we host a dark and cruel side in which our demons lie. If we favor only one of these sides, we repress the other, altering the balance. That is why Jung, in accordance with Taoism and the ontologies of many native peoples around the world, showed that the human psyche is made up of black and white, light and darkness, good and evil, and that it is therefore necessary to take care of both energies. If we fail to do so, the more destructive side ends up imposing itself on the more compassionate side. Environmental ethics must integrate our opposites, consciously confront the collective shadow of our ecocidal impulses, and closely watch our uncontrolled desire to increase our dominion over nature.

Jung mentioned that the shadow is only truly dangerous when we do not pay it due attention, and that recognizing it is the first step in coming to some kind of agreement with it and channeling it toward more creative ends. Confronting the collective shadow helps us to weaken it, to lessen its density, and to gain power over it. This means accepting, first of all, that the collective ecocidal shadow nests in the unconscious fantasy of capitalist societies, according to which the world is an inexhaustible and available source to satisfy our whims. This collective shadow wishes that the living earth has no limits, that it does not demand that we quit, and that we can continue to drink from it as much as we wish—a sort of transfer of our infantile instincts with our mother's breast (Cesarman, 1972). We wish to live as comfortably as possible and to have unrestricted access to the luxuries, goods and services, and all those objects of desire that modern civilization places in front of us. To fulfill this desire we need to disconnect, to be desensitized to the pain of the earth as we allow this desire to flow and circulate freely, relegating to the unconscious the reminder that this urge leads to death. We do not want to know or connect affectively; we have no interest in repressing this desire, and we send everything that is contrary to it to the darkest corners of our mind.

There is another way to understand this ecocidal shadow: that we are aware of the planetary destruction, that there has never been so much information on climate change, that there has never been so much knowledge about the loss of biodiversity and the pollution generated by our consumption habits, and yet, this knowledge does not create an affect in the body, it does not produce meaning. Worse still: it is also possible that a "cynical reason" (Sloterdijk, 2003) prevails, which can be summarized in the following aphorism: "they know very well what they do, but even so, they do it" (Žižek, 2001, p. 61). That is to say, today many of us know that the capitalist lifestyle destroys the fabric of life, and yet, cynically, we continue the lifestyle without changing our consumption habits, wishing to remain immersed in this system.

How can we have a creative, healthy relationship with this ecocidal shadow? How can we come to an agreement with this dark force that drives us toward our own destruction? There is a pressing urgency to deal with this thanatic force. We need to acknowledge and control it by becoming aware that we reproduce this *regime of affectivity* insofar as it faithfully conforms to the desires of the collective shadow that inhabits us. Maintaining a proper relationship with the shadow brings enormous possibility, not only—as Connie Zweig and Jeremiah Abrams (1991, p. 16) put it—to "reduce its inhibitory or destructive power," but also to "release the positive life energy that is trapped within it," as we will see in the next chapter. Building an environmental ethics requires taking advantage of this collective shadow, confronting it and integrating it, to understand that any action in this direction will not lead us immediately and forever to adequate behavior, without contradictions or fissures, and rather to understand that a new *ethos* will end neither in perpetual harmony, nor in perennial reconciliation with the earth, nor in a definitive enlightenment. Instead we will have to skillfully juggle the dialectic of opposites, with ups and downs, with the struggle between dark and light (Hekimian, 2015).

To maintain a healthy relationship with the ecocidal shadow, as James Hillman (1991) observes, means acknowledging what we have hidden, becoming aware of the type of affections constructed by this system in whose bosom we dwell, of the type of thinking that inhabits us, of the thousand ways in which we deceive ourselves, the type of desires we have, and noticing which beings we are capable of harming and destroying in order to obtain those desires. Caring for the shadow, protecting ourselves from its destructive influence—continues the author—sometimes means simply acknowledging it, carrying it, taking it with us, taking charge of it, recognizing our insensitivities, our anesthetics, our cruelty, our most unpleasant facets, in order to reduce its power over life. Suffering, pain, and evil are human aspects that we cannot eliminate. We must build an environmental ethics within this dark dimension, a different *ethos* that mitigates the consequences of the collective shadow, if we want to create another form of sensitive relationship with the bodies of the earth and not succumb to the greatest of dangers.

Recognizing the ecocidal *regime of affectivity* of our time also means responding politically, entering a struggle for the hegemony of affectivities. This struggle must acknowledge our shadow, but also make use of our bodily potential and power, its ability to take charge of its desires, to rekindle its senses, and to create an ethics that protects us from ourselves.

5

The Desire for Life: The Aesthetic Reorganization of Affections

If we let it, capitalism will turn the planet into an inhospitable sphere. Scientific forecasts are getting worse and worse, while social inertia is becoming the norm. Turbulent times await us in this long civilizational decline in which there will likely be further commodification in areas that have so far been spared from the tentacles of the marketplace. Capital is investing and expanding the desert into new territories, where gunpowder demolishes the mountains, oil fields replace the ceiba trees and mercury poisons the springs. This prognosis puts us in an alarming situation, for even a scenario where the industrial system collapses could be worse than the one we are suffering today. Nothing guarantees that the social organization that would follow an abrupt collapse would be better than the current ecocidal, culturicidal, and genocidal system. On the contrary, it is feasible that wars against peoples and their territories will take on faces hitherto unimagined, that more corners of the planetary geography will experience renewed authoritarian regimes, that the generous world will be displaced by the withering, consumption, and inhibition of life. This apocalyptic scene could become irreversible if we let it, if we are not able to stop this suicidal odyssey, if we are not prepared to dream of a less petty destiny. Everything really depends on the political response of the peoples. We have no other option but to prevent "the disoriented bird from flying in the direction opposite to abundance," as Payeras puts it, preparing the ground with actions that weave other forms of community in connection with the relationships that make life possible.

If this political reaction is to truly challenge this dystopian scenario, it must address, in unison with the economic, social, and technological dimension, the sensitive network and the symbolic engine that gives support and meaning to the entirety of contemporary living. Of course, the struggle must include profound changes to the current system of accumulation in order to build many other worlds based on cooperation, solidarity, and reciprocity, but this would clearly be incomplete without a struggle to change the affective regime that shapes the social order of our times. Preparing the ground means undertaking the difficult task of deconstructing the *regime of affectivity* that governs sensitivity and organizes the affections; radically questioning how the sensitive order is distributed and the strategies by which aesthetic tastes are created, as well as the way in which this regime is inscribed in the body, colonizes the senses, and configures the affective rails and modes of perception. If we want to jump off the highway destined for the abyss, we must begin to denormalize the desiring ecology, the plastic words and anthropocentric discourses, and all forms of sensibility that turn the vivacity of the world into a collection of inert, soulless things. We shall undertake a political struggle that seeks to antagonize ontologically, epistemically, and ethically the affective regime that both the dominant and the dominated share, and without which it would be impossible to continue reproducing the current ecocidal model.

Needless to say, this political struggle can hardly be carried out through professional politicians, parties, laws, institutions, or elections—a space where the anthropocentric metaphysics is reproduced over and over. It must instead appeal to other modes of organization beyond the State and the market, where it is more plausible to reorganize affective relations, and to make an embodied politics that understands that the struggle for power is fought in the territory-bodies. We insist: there are many terrains in which to start a fight with this system, but one of particular importance is the field of affectivity. It is a space where narcissistic commercialized relationships, disaffection, a lack of empathy, and the insensitivity that enables cruelty are created. If we do not work on the symbolic and affective order, the old order will emerge in any new order as a symptom, replicating its ominous ecologies. Avoiding the latency of the affective regime means taking charge, recognizing the collective shadow, and carrying out symbolic operations that go to the heart of the problem, making new and creative ethical and aesthetic irruptions that are capable of decolonizing bodies and dehegemonizing affections.

Dismantling the bodily conditions that enable the hegemony of the *regime of affectivity*, whose purpose is to structure the emotional economy and establish the system of sensibilities and anesthetics that are essential for modern capitalism to carry out its predatory work, entails reviving the senses, creating different forms of *environmental affectivity*, and awakening to active participation with the ground-body that sustains us, the air-body from which we draw our breath, the bluish sensitive atmosphere in which we are immersed. If it is true that this system "needs to build a «regime of the sensitive», a certain consensus—as Gramsci would say—regarding what *a body can do*" (Castro-Gómez, 2018, p. 296), there is no way to dispute hegemony if we do not try to banish this regime from our bodies and territorialize instead an *environmental affectivity* compatible with the self-organizations of the *multiplicities* that we inhabit and inhabit us. The *regime of affectivity* has fashioned a lair from which springs the meaning of human acts, offering support to a form of relationship that excludes our ontological understanding as bodies among bodies, and instituting instead instrumental relationships between subjects and objects. Therefore, any political uprising in favor of life must consider the mode of affective organization and the bodily forms that the system seeks to produce, as well as the various sensitive ways in which we can escape to build other relational affectivities.

The construction of power, of the things we are capable of when we recognize ourselves as bodies that live among other bodies, will depend, at first, on dismantling the hegemonic *regime of affectivity*, and then on an awakening to the power of the body itself. Only this operation will be able to support suspending the way we do things today; to give symbolic structure to an interruption of the modern way of understanding the world; to allow something unexpected to emerge, not from nothing, but from what was brewing in the heart of peoples and collectives in their processes of resistance to the growth of the desert created by this indolent system.

Counter-Hegemonies of Desire

The environmental *ethos* cannot be constructed without first taking seriously the sophisticated way in which capitalism creates meaning and mobilizes desire. As psychoanalysis has explained, capital has the immense capacity to direct the desire of the population and the signifiers of the unconscious. Through sophisticated devices, it ensures that goods are not consumed for their utility, but for the enjoyment created by the experience of their consumption to the extent that they fill life with meaning. Think of Coca-Cola advertising: perhaps the best example of how the system works. Coca-Cola does not sell a soft drink, not carbonated water with sugar and coloring, but a sense of life—let us remember its slogans: "Choose your life," "Live the sensation," and "Open happiness." As Žižek (2012) explains, commodities are not simply objects that we buy and consume: they are "something more," they contain a "surplus" of meaning, which is ultimately the object of desire. In other words, commodities are desired not because we want them as goods or services, but because we identify with them insofar as they fill our ontological void with meaning, even if only partially. Well, just as Coca-Cola does, capitalism creates a symbolic and affective order that shapes social and socio-environmental relations. It cunningly manages to make us want to keep living within its coordinates, because without them we would lose the meaning provided by consumption and would be forced to confront our own ontological emptiness (Žižek, 2001).

This vacuum, not filled by *environmental knowledge*, as Leff (2021) observes, is eventually occupied by the meanings produced by the system. We must remember that this urban-industrial civilization allows the majority to ignore how to produce or search for food, how to build a shelter, how to make clothes, how to transform energy, and, in general, it allows them to ignore how to link their body with the natural cycles and the dark night of the cosmos. In other words, it makes it possible to live without the *environmental knowledge* that made us human, creating a void, a lack that seeks to be filled by the sensitive regime of capitalism, which, as St. Augustine says, makes us love more what should be loved less and love less what should be loved more. Our disoriented civilization suffers from a heart that loves more what jeopardizes the conditions that make life possible and loves less everything it depends on to exist. The question then is how we can bring forth a desire in the unconscious that is not co-opted by capital, which does not make us suffer from a disordered heart, but that brings forth a desire *before* life, a desire *for* life.

We believe that the *regime of affections* cannot be fought with a rational critique—as proposed by a rationalist environmental ethics in the manner of Callicott[1]—and even less through guilt—as proposed by environmentalist discourses that suggest saving the world through changes in consumption—but by entering into a direct competition for desire. Since drive is inherent to capitalism, and capitalism stimulates our "desire to desire," as Žižek (2005) holds, there is no path but to dispute desire with the system. We need to play in its own court and snatch its hegemony as the machine that guides desire. Desire is not fatal; capitalism does not own it once and for all. It is disputed turf. Therefore, there is no other option than to fight for this desire, and, amid destruction, to awaken our desiring activity toward life. Let us consider again Coca-Cola, the perfect commodity according to the Slovenian philosopher. This drink has the property that the more we drink it, instead of satiating our desire, the thirstier we become. What does Coca-Cola do then? It stimulates our desire to continue desiring (Žižek, 2012). Well, then we must follow this same logic to compete in its own ground, creating other imaginary identifications to constantly reproduce life as a drive. We need to displace the identification of meaning attached to our consumption of commodities and reorient it toward a *drive for life*.

A pragmatic example of this idea are agroecology's social processes of multiplication, specifically peasant to peasant pedagogy, as we explained more broadly in our previous work (Giraldo, 2018, 103–21). This way in which popular organizations in the countryside work makes agroecology grow by contagion, by example and by stimulating desire. People get excited when they visit another family's plot and see the results of diversification, the advantages of ecological practices, and the benefits of ecotechnologies. Their desire to live agroecologically awakens. But this does not happen through guilt or by making people feel bad about sustaining the system of death that destroys us—capitalism is skilled at making us feel sad and responsible for the problems caused by capitalism itself—but because it shows a good life and a green environment where birds sing and butterflies flutter over the many flowers of the landscape, where we eat diverse foods, and where life is different than in the system of dependencies, debt, and poison that has desolated the fields and expelled its inhabitants. Everything works through contagion, by moving desire. When agroecology is good and life is beautiful, the food is much better than at the supermarket; dwellings are built with materials from the earth, more thermal and beautiful than concrete constructions and the matchboxes people are crammed into in cities. In the end, this life is more desirable than the life in cities' urban belts, with overcrowded subways and buses, exploitative bosses, and miserly wages. This is a good example of how to compete for desire against the system. If we are creative, we can renounce the joy provided by capitalist symbolization.

Agroecology is merely an illustrative case of those political proposals, of environmental ethics based on contact and environmental knowledge, as we have been discussing. It is not an ethics based on moral judgments or obligations, but on an environmental *ethos* in which people take charge of their desire in the face of life, and by sheer disinterest cease to yield to the desires imposed by capitalism. Contrary to the capital-centrist idea that capitalism has totalized all social relations (Gibson-Graham, 1997), we see instead that the system is increasingly inefficient in symbolically and affectively structuring reality, and that a growing number of people are trying to identify with agroecology, permaculture, intentional communities, friendly exchanges, and spirituality.

We are imagining a political response to destruction based on the drive of conatus: a fundamental category for our analytical reflection. Let us recall that Spinoza called conatus the drive to continue to exist, the intention that life should continue to be life. It is that drive to exist, that force of wanting to go on being that is inherent in every expression of life. The conatus is a volition, a will to be preserved; an appetite, an appetency for life; a thirst for existence; and an active affirmation of a body to continue existing. And at the same time, it is an impulse to resist any manifestation that threatens the possibility of remaining (Spinoza, 2011). Well, an important characteristic that we observe in the popular uprisings against extractivist projects, pollution, climate change, and environmental injustice is that the conatus emerges almost like a cry. It is the rejection of death and the affirmation of life which is, in a way, a vindication of that primordial desire, of that appetite for life, which emerges—as an animal defending itself against its predator—in the face of a specific threat. Although the system has turned us against the nature of the conatus impulse, as Madelin (2016) reminds us, the desire for life emerges through contingent processes in which peoples make a political decision regarding a particular situation. There is no universalism, there is no social class, and there is no culture better endowed than any other to respond to the subtraction of life. In the face of each contingency, each concrete threat, and each affront, every people take a stand and seek a particular response to this desire for life. The peoples are taking charge of the suffering caused by capitalism's will to power in multiple ways, with creative strategies, using pain and death anxiety in their favor.

Anger and even hatred play a fundamental role in these types of political responses. In many politicized bodies—individual or organized—that defend life and territory, a feeling of "empathetic injustice" emanates, in which a certain discomfort, impotence, and sadness arises first in the face of pain and environmental injustice, to later transform into anger and indignation. This emotional response to the war against the territories usually helps trigger the conditions to act in "defense of life"—as social movements commonly call it— because instead of paralyzing and immobilizing they are a great motivator for standing against a specific threat (Toro, 2021).

Undoubtedly, one of the biggest contradictions of the death project we live in is that it activates the life drive: it makes angry bodies fill with conatus. The drive for life, the desire for life, emerges when the ecologies of death become stronger. The peoples, by resisting actions that threaten their existence and other living beings, express their profound desire for life to continue to be life. The strokes of death imposed by the capitalist project in concrete attacks stimulate the peoples to awaken their empathic injustice, to recover their power to act, and, paradoxically, to catalyze the organization of collective action around life. A common pattern in movements that defend territory in our time is that in the face of danger the objects of desire transform, and it becomes a cause for the deepest roots of life. The psychoanalyst tradition has taught that this could not be otherwise, because, as Lacan thought, we desire what we lack. That is why the lack of life energizes the impulse of the desire for life, moving from negativity to affirmation, from anguish to action, and from the loss of land, water, mountains, or jungle to ethical action to save the blessing that is in danger.

Once again we rely on psychoanalysis to understand the ethics arising from these processes. Lacan (2007) thought that ethics arises when the subject no longer gives in to the desire of the other and takes charge of their own desire. This means that one is ethical when one stops giving in to the desires imposed by capitalism, when one stops needing it as a symbolic structure. The question posed by this psychoanalyst is to know if we act in accordance with the desire that inhabits us, which could be reinterpreted—at the risk of de-Lacanizing too much—as asking if we act in accordance with the conatus desire that vibrates within us. This question refers to our body, to our most intimate desire. It is an ethical question that inquires about the original desire for life and about the responsibility for our capacity to do things. We cannot forget that denying this desire has made it easier for inadequate ideas[2] to be inoculated by the *potestas* of capitalism, turning off the power, leading to the loss of power itself. Subsumed in the dominant affective regimes, riddled with inadequate ideas and the disconnections they impose on us, we have been dispossessed of responsibility, compromising our vital power. However, in the face of the danger, an ethical political choice has arisen in many collectives, which, of course, is not an obligation or a moral, but a will. It is a conatus through which we reveal the deep desire for life that inhabits us.

What has been emerging in different parts of the world is a call to reorganize and restore the order of love. If the *regime of affectivity* had disorganized the *ordo amoris*, causing the disordered heart to give importance to what has no value, and downplaying the importance of what we vitally require to continue to exist, an appetite for life has emerged as a political response, an energy of conatus conservation opposed to the ecologies of violence and aggression determined to take the life out of life. Within our collective shadows and our refusal to be sensitive to the sensibility of other beings, an ecology of love has come to sprout as a kind of rebellious fissure in the frenetic death drive of capitalism. This ecology of eros acts by contagion of desire. It spreads like a nutrient that flows and is distributed through a network of erotic ramifications, showing that the system is not totalitarian and that there is always a gap, an inability to subsume it all. An ecology of collective conatus is silently emerging in these cracks, trying to reorganize the affective order altered by the imaginations and desires that reproduce the plundering of the living planet.

We cannot understand environmental ethics without eros, without the dimension of love that all *ethos* carries with it. Together with the collective thanatos, there is a generative, poietic eros, capable of creating—as Eric Fromm (2000) thought—a network that produces more love. Just as there is an ecology of expansive cruelty that stimulates desire for that which denies life, there are also erotic rhizomatic loops, which, as in any process of positive feedback, amplify the desire for life. To ignore these collective movements, and to think that only thanatic ecologies exist, is to give greater force to the project of death that consumes the earth. Amid ecological ruin, dynamic links of different kinds are springing up, which are organized around this *thirst for life that* generates more *thirst for life*. These are loving networks that understand that love is not passive but active, that seek the right action through a mutually enriching connection with the living soil. These are people who devote themselves in the hope of producing love in the beloved world and are concerned with establishing right relationships in constant correspondence between themselves and the inhabited space.

We must therefore remove the *regime of affectivity* of death that makes us enjoy destruction; we must dismantle this sensitive order that causes us suffering. And for this we must enter into a contest for desire with this system. Our resource at hand is the most original desire: the insatiable need for life that inhabits us. We will have to resort to this essential drive for life to prevail over death, through the weaving of erotic nets. As the mythical story of Ares and Aphrodite reminds us, only love can defeat war (Pineda, 2014). However, these processes of love for the living earth are not built out of guilt—so deeply rooted in our Judeo-Christian heritage—but out of a thirst for life, a political decision in the face of a concrete threat, often driven by empathetic injustice: an affection that stems from the unequal ecological distribution of the evils of devastation.

Aesthetics of Environmental Affectivity

As we have suggested in our discussion of environmental knowledge, aesthetics is the essential ontological condition of environmental ethics. There is no possibility of resisting the will to power of capitalism and its technological platform, nor the feasibility of preparing the ground for a new order, if we do not create an adequate aesthetic environment to change the position in which peoples' perceptions participate; if we do not create an atmosphere conducive for the body to develop its full power. The ethics of life is also an aesthetic, because the coupling between our human body and the other bodies we encounter depends on a choice of what is attractive, on a sensual and erotic intonation to know how to choose what is appropriate to life. Therefore, restoring the proper order of love depends on a proper adjustment of the senses with the environment, and on recovering the aesthetic bias of our evolutionary lineage so we are attracted to what is good for life and reject all that is harmful to it.

We stress once again: the choice of what is good, of what fits into the fundamentals of life, depends on our aesthetic prejudice, on our capacity to choose what is attractive, to be seduced by what is charming. As Spinoza (2011, p. 223) said, "we do not try, want, crave or desire something because we judge it to be good; on the contrary, we judge something to be good because we try, want, crave and desire it." That is, we judge something to be good because we are attracted to it, because we approach it through attraction; and, on the contrary, we judge something to be bad or unprofitable because we feel repulsion, an intuition of alienation; we consider it inconvenient because our conatus tells us that we should reject it, as if it were poison. Therefore, in an uncluttered love, we would prefer and find desirable everything that nourishes and preserves us, while we would shy away from, and in fact find it utter folly to love, that which puts us on the verge of collapse.

Environmental affectivity, in these times so threatening to the habitability of many beings, means recovering this sense of what is good for the place because our senses tell us so. It means regenerating the sense of proportion, of beauty and its association with what is "good." A feature of environmental knowledge, as we discussed earlier, is that the power to act increases when the life experience is inscribed in small-scale environments, and on the contrary, the capacity to act tends to decrease when living in larger-scale spaces. This is why living in well-proportioned places where direct contact with the beings of the earth is possible promotes the mobilization of environmental empathy, which is usually not cultivated in social designs of gigantic scales, where civilization allows the majority to ignore the environmental knowledge most essential for survival. Recovering contact is a prerequisite for activating our evolutionary memory, reviving our aesthetic biases—thanks to which we prefer the sensation of life to that of death—and being seduced by the pleasure of what is good for life while rejecting the displeasure of poison.

Aesthetics is indispensable for life, because we depend on sensations and perceptions to survive, as they provide guidance to know how to find what suits the body, and the criteria to choose the right mixtures to fit the place. Good aesthetic compositions and ethics are closely related, because in the course of the long evolutionary history, our senses have been guided to feel attraction toward the beautiful, pleasant, and desirable; a particular conatus has been created to resonate and tune into certain aesthetic arrangements. Thanks to aesthetics we can connect with other bodies once we train our senses and develop an attentiveness, an appreciative listening, and a deep observation of them. When we refine the intensity of the senses, we can awaken to their need, to their taste, to their desire, or their suffering. Sensory modulation is the resource that helps us to know what kind of actions should be taken to make appropriate compositions in the place where we are, and the tool that allows us to shape a common sense that weaves affective rails facilitating connection, communication, and sensitive openness to understand what a good or a bad encounter between bodies means.

Aesthetics is the language of the earth, in which the invisibility of the scent of flowers, the rhythms of birdsong, and the intensity of the colors of shrubby leaves all participate. All the gestures, murmurs, chromatic combinations, and perfumes of biological and geological forms, shaped by aesthetic patterns made with their own symmetries, contours, and rhythms, offer us subtle guides on how to inhabit among the diverse types of bodies. The sensitive earth calls us to connect with it through a language made of sensations, emotional paths, signs, and aesthetic messages. Each specific space, be it a tropical forest, a temperate savannah, a rocky mountain or a boreal bog, has its own signs, its own aesthetic language and specific emotionality. All beings and landscapes have the capacity to communicate through a language of sensitivities, empathies, and affections. Through sensations, through messages tailored for specific perceivers, each creature displays its capacity for attraction or repulsion, for creating in another body a form of affection (Mandoki, 2013). And it is there, in the aesthetic exuberance, that the earth touches us, that we are summoned to tune our senses with the web of paths to make a good place among them.

However, a disorder of love made us fragile and eroded our ability to connect with that aesthetic. It made us unable to see the beauty of life, isolated us from the stars, the chickens, and the marigold. It made us think of ourselves so far away from the ladybugs, so disconnected from the hummingbird and the cricket's song, so cut off from what sustains and nourishes life. Even so, the living landscape that lives even beneath the asphalt we walk on patiently awaits the awakening of our senses so that we can reconnect with the sensation of the perfume of the damp earth, of the first visible star at nightfall, and of the return to our deepest aesthetic preferences. The world, with its sensitive language, speaks fruitlessly to our sensory embodiment, inviting it to re-engage with the voice of the wind, the roar of the water, the crackle of the fire, and the silence of the ground. The sobbing of the earth, sometimes expressed with hurricanes, sometimes with fires over savannahs and jungles, or with the threat of extinction of the koala, is an urgent call to awaken our senses and re-tune our affections and thoughts to the tastes of the earth, water, and air.

To awaken one's senses is to free the body from anthropocentric codes, from utilitarian languages, from the levity of imposed desires, and to invigorate that old forgotten sense that teaches that what is good for the body and the soul must also be pleasing to the experience of smell, taste, skin, hearing, and sight. To understand that the features of ethics are aesthetic, and that therefore, all we need is to lend our senses to the manifestations of acoustic habitats, to the revelation of the composition of clouds, and to the warning of fragrances contrary to the liking of our olfactory glands. We need to trust our sensory bodies again and respond affectively to the subtle indications of the earth's tongue. If the earth empathizes with us, if sentient beings resonate with our emotions and feelings, if permanently the other interwoven bodies are welcoming and echoing our affective state, then we must trust that the living landscape is telling us what "is right" with its peculiar aesthetic registers. To understand this, we only need to regain faith in our senses and their ability to inform our ethical actions, to let ourselves be guided by the aesthetics of nature through our sensory interaction, and thus know what is best for the place.

But what is missing to recover this aesthetic sense so lost in our time? The land itself tells us: more and more aesthetics of life. As our environment changes, as we increase our contact with the cycles of life, and as we plant forests of flowers and gardens of orchards, our perceptions open up at the same pace: our withered senses emerge. Transformed places, where the dragonfly, the pollen, the nectar, and the salamander return, have the immense power to modify our bodies and enliven our senses. By interacting and getting in close contact with the environment, often with the guidance of someone who is already sensitive, we can be amazed at how our perceptions are awakened. Places where diversity, multiplicity, and love sprout have the immense capacity to pollinate us, affect our bodies, and clear our sensibility. They exert their power by inhabiting us, by providing us with the relational, symbiotic, and affective senses forgotten by our disoriented modernity.

We have been privileged to experience this sensitive transformation. Several years ago we had the opportunity to move from the megalopolises of Bogota and Mexico City to a peaceful country setting in the Chiapas highlands. We first lived in an austere cabin lost among the canopy of pines and oaks, and then we built our home in a small wetland made of grasses and chamomiles, surrounded by small hills. This experience changed our life completely: it gave us the opportunity to be, the gift of a space to see the different forms of life daily and to enjoy their perfection and beauty. Two days ago an eagle glided just a few meters above our heads, an experience that would have been unthinkable until a few years ago. We remember that our sensation during the first night in the solitary cabin was to feel intimidated by the darkness, deeply amazed by the night full of stars, but above all because we heard for the first time the silence of the night—an overwhelming silence, an unknown calm, colored by the cicadas that lull us to sleep. Little by little our perception changed, and we enhanced our amazement at the intelligence of the spiders, refined our appreciation for the smell of rain, and for that magical moment when the September showers cease and the mist appears in the forest. Changing our urban habits meant having the sensation that everything was happening before our senses.

Little by little, our ears were tuned, and we learned to distinguish the different barks of dogs and identify when birds talk, argue, fight or play; we learned to differentiate when a dog barks at a horse, a human, and another dog; as well as to understand the tonalities of some birds' songs. Living in these new places awakened in us the ability to sense a frost, to worry every day about the well-being of the seedbeds and small crops, and to feel a very intimate impulse to take permanent care of the land. We were amazed by this surprising miracle in which we just had to add water to a seed and wait for pumpkins, garlic, potatoes, coriander or tomatoes to be born from it. We fell in love with compost and worms. They give you the awareness that everything is susceptible to becoming soil; they give you the gift of showing you how the conditions of the existence of each thing change, and that each small death is actually part of the cycle of life. Taking care of the orchard helped us develop a subtle perception of the seedlings and to develop the environmental empathy thanks to which you can sense their need and respond empathetically to their desire. The contact with the soil made us marvel at the conatus of the plants, to realize that, despite their fragility, many of them grow profusely in difficult conditions. Harvesting rainwater and cleaning it in a biofilter gave us the awareness of our impact on the world, and, in general, our daily life among the site's rich fauna provided us with the opportunity not only for an aesthetic enjoyment unknown to our bodies, but the ability to enliven and relocate our senses and affections.

Our experience has made us reaffirm the belief that ontological and spiritual changes are pragmatic, that environmental ethics can only be a correlate of an ontological transformation, and that it cannot happen without contact and without a territory. Environmental ethics is a discovery, something that occurs, but a place is necessary for it to happen. For this reason, a true environmental ethics cannot do without the struggle for the earth, so that people can transform it ethically and aesthetically. The problem is that current urban spaces tend to limit the sensitive and affective experience with the living earth, because they have been built to facilitate the circulation of goods and the exploitation of labor, to make viable the ignorance of environmental knowledge, and to make it possible for their inhabitants to ignore the ecological footprint of their modes of production and consumption. The comforts of urban life lead us toward disconnection as we relate to a world made not of wild nature but of modified nature. The design of cities with their enormous energy expenditure and dependence on land clearance makes it difficult to practice an environmental ethic. Its artificial atmospheres, its shopping malls, its light pollution, the infernal exposure of commercial propaganda, its airplanes sailing across the sky, or its cell phones invading our intimate life make it easy to disconnect our sensitive experience from the organic earth; make it so that places are nothing more but narcissistic reflection of our signs (Abram, 1996), and that our Baconian affectivity is still determined to dominate the forces of the earth. Of course, there are many urban people with the sensibility and desire for life, and there are enormous efforts to revitalize cities, but the way of living forced by the layout of large cities, and the disproportion that megacities have reached, makes it difficult to recover the sense of proportionality with concrete acts, and makes it difficult to couple the sensory experience with the living conditions.

Even so, we will have to free ourselves from this yoke and imagine creative aesthetic interventions to revitalize small and proportionate agglomerations in reclaimed and poetically inhabited lands. We shall rebuild other civilizing modes made of environmental knowledge where more people can create an *environmental affectivity*, a renewed loving ethos that includes transformed, greened cities. Given that places inhabit us, that spaces determine our sensibilities, our emotional colorations, our moods, and our thoughts, we have no choice but to create aesthetic spaces that facilitate the reconnection with our senses, and that allow us to trust again in the ethics that teach us the bonds, interactions and redistributions of the organic land. These aesthetic creations will require not only aesthetic interventions of a technical nature, but also aesthetic interventions of a linguistic nature. In unison with the political struggle for the desire for life, we must navigate against the current of capitalist symbolization in which the dominant metaphysics is repeated over and over by constructing an epistemo-aesthesis that creates other imaginaries, other symbolic orders consonant with the sense of the earth, more akin to these loving attempts to reorganize the world based on the conditions of life, as many peoples and collectives around the world are doing.

We must remember that there is a profound relationship between the word and the body, both in perception and in the unconscious, that we are made in the realm of the word, and that this word is much more than human. Our verbal articulations are composed in their depths by a language made up of multiple sensitives gravitating in the terrestrial autoformations. If we do not claim in our enunciations the belonging to the place and the correspondence with the beings that allow us to be among them, we will be condemned to exile and to forgetting the memory of this thin film of life suspended in the cosmos and illuminated by a twinkling star. The way in which our body and our senses connect or disconnect from the earth that we are will depend to a great extent on the capacity to symbolize the world, to name it and to poetically express it in language. And by poeticize we are thinking of the collective ability to weave symbols that open the world to the senses in an attitude of permanent amazement that makes us remember, at every moment, that there is nothing more beautiful than our celestial home. In the end, we will have to look for many ways to magically and poetically name everything that exists, to compose signs that allow us to understand that we are corporealities inter-being, and to form a powerful discourse capable of emancipating us from the violence of signifying a disenchanted land, and to guide the experience of daily life according to an earthly language.

One day, we will finally understand that establishing an aesthetic ethics and an environmental affectivity is not optional: it is the only possibility in the face of this vertiginous hurricane of ruins and debris that, in its excess, is dangerously approaching the abyss.

Notes

Chapter 1

1. For this reason, as Val Plumwood (2002, 2005) has said, environmental thought is not a type of knowledge focused exclusively on defending non-human nature—plants, animals, ecosystems—but a type of political ontology that defends the repressed aspects of duality: affectivity, sensitivity, intuition, spirituality, femininity, the body, and all those attributes associated with "nature," placed in an inferior level and therefore susceptible to being exploited and dominated.
2. For further discussion of the relationship between Spinoza's ethics and deep ecology, see Naess (1980).
3. For example, the Tzeltal peoples of Chiapas, Mexico, have the concept of *ch'ulel*, which according to López-Intzín, is the heart-soul-spirit-consciousness that animates and energizes everything. According to these peoples, every being has *ch'ulel*: "Human beings, plants, animals, minerals, hills, rivers, and everything that exists in the universe has *Ch'ulel—ch'ulelal*. Therefore everything has its own language and speaks, feels, cries, and its heart thinks" (López-Intzín, 2015, p. 190).
4. In Eastern wisdom, Buddhist monk Nāgārjuna (2004) has a phrase that beautifully summarizes this idea: "If there were identity between the word and its object, the word 'fire' would burn the mouth."
5. We have only explored the first of the Abhidharma books, which is that of the body. The rest are about the mental aggregates, in which, according to the doctrine, there is also no basis for finding an "I."
6. The power of Argentine philosopher José Luis Grosso's voice and thoughts encouraged us to think of "the environment" as a question of bodies among bodies.

Chapter 2

1. Francisco Varela introduces the neologism *enactive*—in-action—to assert that cognition is not a passive but an active process. Cognition is literally "an act" in which each organism conjures a world that is meaningful to it.
2. We cite this classic experiment because it is illustrative, but not without questioning the ethical basis underlying this type of animal research.
3. There are numerous examples of empathic capacity among animal species. It is worth noting an experiment conducted by De Waal himself and collaborators, in which a capuchin monkey accompanied by another individual of his species was given a choice between two kinds of objects that were interchangeable for food. The first object represented food for him and his companion—the "prosocial" option—while selecting the second object meant that his companion would not receive food—the "selfish" option. The capuchins that participated in the experiment tended to choose the "prosocial" option, which according to De Waal shows the interest of these primates in the welfare of their conspecifics, especially if there is a strong bond between them.
4. An example of the human willingness to constantly read the moods of others can be found in a study cited by Batson (2009). In this 1976 research by Sagi and Hoffman, two-day-old infants were presented with two recordings of infant cries: one cry was synthetic and the other real, but the infants only reacted to and became emotionally affected by the recording of the real cry. The researchers interpreted this reaction as evidence of "rudimentary empathy" (Batson, 2009, p. 6).
5. This perspective reminds us of Adam Smith (1941, p. 33): "When we see a stroke aimed and just ready to fall upon the leg or arm of another person, we naturally shrink and draw back our own leg or our own arm; and when it does fall, we feel it in some measure, and are hurt by it as well as the sufferer. The mob, when they are gazing at a dancer on the slack rope, naturally writhe and twist and balance their own bodies, as they see him do, and as they feel that they themselves must do if in his situation."

6   Anthropomorphism and its relationship to empathy has been studied extensively by Claire Parkinson (2019).

7   A classic example of how there is no context-independent human nature is that of children raised by wild animals. There is a famous case of two girls from northern India who were found in 1922 in the "bosom of a family of wolves who had raised them in complete isolation from all human contact." The girls could not walk on two feet, but they moved quickly on all four limbs. They did not speak, their faces remained expressionless, they had nocturnal habits, only wanted to eat raw meat, and rejected human contact. One of the girls survived for ten more years—the other died soon after the encounter—and eventually changed her eating habits and walked on two feet, "although she always resorted to running on all fours when moved by urgency. She never spoke properly, although she did use a few words. The family of the Anglican missionary who rescued and cared for her, as well as the other people who knew her somewhat intimately, never felt she was truly human" (Maturana and Varela, 2003, pp. 85–6). This case clearly shows that each environment has different teaching processes that activate and lead to the development of human capacities and skills in different ways.

Chapter 3

1   Aesthetics is also concerned with "the ugly," "the horrible," "the kitsch," "the baroque," "the *ch'ixi*," and "the disjointed." In this essay we will focus on the relationship between the intrinsic beauty of the patterns of life and ethics.

2   Illich tacitly alludes to Schumacher's (2011) classic work *Small Is Beautiful*: "Kohr remains a prophet today because even the humanist theorists for whom small is beautiful have not discovered that true beauty and goodness is not a matter of size or even of the dimensions of intensity, but of proportion" (Illich, 1997, p. 2).

3 The association between aesthetic criteria and the orientation of what is "good" is inscribed in the language of many peoples. In Nahuatl, for example, the beautiful—*cualtzin*—is rooted in the good—*cualli*—while in P'urhepecha, *sesi jasï*—the beautiful—is derived from *sesi*—the good (Alvarado, 2020). In Spanish, meanwhile, the word *bello* comes from the Latin *bellus*, a contraction of *benulus*, which in turn is a diminutive of *bonus*, meaning "good" or "beautiful."

4 Information provided by Chahim Huet Macz, the Guatemalan Q'eqchi' agronomist.

Chapter 4

1 It is important to clarify, as Pierre Madelin (2020) warns, that cruelty is a matter of the human condition. We are not saying that vernacular communities only have numinous aspects while modern communities only have the ominous. In hunter-gatherer and horticultural societies, there has been patriarchy, slavery, torture, anthropophagy, and war. And we cannot ignore the fact that, with all its imperfections, modern society is the only one that has promulgated the idea of human rights, abolished slavery, and challenged gender inequalities like never before. All of the above is incomplete, of course, but it is necessary to recognize the virtues of modernity and to emphasize that vernacular societies are not free of the darkest passions.

2 For a comprehensive study on empathic disability and its association with malice, see Baron-Cohen (2012).

3 In an account gathered by Victoria Uribe (2018, p. 116), when a survivor of this massacre asked one of the perpetrators how he felt when the victims begged him not to kill them, he answered: "No, it's nothing, it's like … the chickens … an animal is a living being, it has life … And then when you kill them, that is, when you are going to eat them, you take their life away from them. And then, just like a human

being, it also has life, the same as animals. Killing a human being, a person, is like killing a chicken. That is like killing an animal."

4   For a comprehensive study on the link between the Jewish Holocaust and animalization, see Patterson (2002).

5   Words, of course, have multiple facets. They can be used in multiple ways. The important thing here is to understand how words are intertwined with acts, and how they are intimately linked to cruelty.

6   By poetic significance we are alluding to an attitude of wonder and respect. As we have expressed elsewhere, "poetry is an attitude towards the world. If capitalist modernity has reduced nature to merchandise, to resources, and to codes of economic value, closing the world and limiting its understanding, poetry is the tool we have left to walk precisely in the opposite direction … Poetry frees us from the violent echoes of occupation that modernity has created and brings us back to aesthetically and respectfully see and listen to the miracle of life" (Noguera and Giraldo, 2017, pp. 90–1).

Chapter 5

1   The rationalist proposal supported by Callicott's positive science, one of the major referents of Anglo-Saxon environmental ethics (Soto-Torres, 2020, p. 98), is quite revealing in this quote: "The commitment to science and rationality implicit in the construction of a theory of environmental ethics is a commitment to reach an agreement through persuasion. It works more or less as follows. I say: here are the facts about nature and human nature provided by the best and most recent efforts of scientific research. And here are the ways in which they could be morally integrated. If you disagree, show me my error and I will adopt your view; or, if you are unable to find any fault with my argument, then you adopt mine. If we both remain open-minded, committed to truth and reason, then at some point we will arrive at the same conclusion … and try to act accordingly" (Callicott, 2006, p. 106).

2. By "inadequate ideas" Spinoza meant the incomplete, confusing ideas, of which we only know their consequences, but not their causes. When one operates within inadequate ideas, one is acting within the world of passions—of suffering and passivity—living under *potestas*, that is, suffering the will of another, prisoners of "external" power, being controlled and separated from our own *potential*—"inner" power. For a detailed explanation of Spinozian thought, see Deleuze (1978, 1980).

Bibliography

Abram, D. (1996). The spell of the sensuous: Perception and language in a more-than human world. Nueva York: Vintage.

Agamben, G. (2017). Homo sacer. El poder soberano y la nuda vida I. San Cristóbal de Las Casas: cideci/unitierra.

Alemán, T. (2016). Vivir para conocer, conocer para vivir: a propósito de campesinos y científicos. LEISA, 32(1), 5–7.

Alvarado, P. (2020). La politicidad de habitar desde la dimensión sensible. Bajo el Volcán, 1(1), 131–51.

Ángel Maya, A. (1996). El reto de la vida. Ecosistema y cultura. Bogotá: Ecofondo.

Arnau, J. (2017). Budismo esencial. Madrid: Alianza.

Austin, J. L. (1990). Cómo hacer cosas con palabras. Barcelona: Paidós.

Baron-Cohen, S. (2012). Empatía cero: Nueva teoría de la crueldad. Madrid: Alianza.

Bataille, G. (1987). La parte maldita. Barcelona: Icaria.

Batson, C. D. (2009). These things called empathy: Eight related but distinct phenomena. In J. Decety y W. Ickes (Eds.), The social neuroscience of empathy (pp. 3–15). Cambridge: MIT Press.

Beauvoir, S. (1981). El segundo sexo. Buenos Aires: Siglo XX.

Blaser, M. (2009). Political ontology: Cultural studies without 'cultures'? Cultural Studies, 23(5–6), 873–96.

Bookchin, M. (1990). The philosophy of social ecology essays on dialectical naturalism. Montreal: Black Rose.

Borja, M. (2018). Tzuultaq'a: defensa territorial, diferencia radical y derecho a la existencia entre los mayas q'eqchi'. Master of Science in Natural Resources and Rural Development Thesis, El Colegio de la Frontera Sur, San Cristóbal de Las Casas, Mexico.

Bourdieu, P. (2016). La distinción: criterio y bases sociales del gusto. Madrid: Taurus.

Callicot, B. (2006). En busca de una ética ambiental. In T. Kwiatkoska y J. Issa (Comps.), Los caminos de la ética ambiental: una antología de textos contemporáneos (pp. 85–159). Mexico: Plaza y Valdés.

Capra, F. (1998). La trama de la vida. Barcelona: Anagrama.
Carver, C. S. y Harmon-Jones, E. (2009). Anger is an approach-related affect: Evidence and implications. Psychol Bull, 135(2), 183–204.
Cassirer, E. (1944). An essay on man. An introduction to a philosophy of human culture. New Haven: Yale University Press.
Castro-García, O. (2009). Jakob von Uexküll: El concepto de Umwelt y el origen de la biosemiótica. PhD Thesis in Philosophy, Universidad Autónoma de Barcelona.
Castro-Gómez, S. (2018). Revoluciones sin sujeto: Slavoj Žižek y crítica historicismo postmoderno. Mexico: Akal.
Cesarman, F. (1972). Ecocidio: estudio psicoanalítico de la destrucción del medio ambiente. Mexico: Joaquín Mortiz.
Chayanov, A. V. (1974). La organización de la unidad económica campesina. Buenos Aires: Nueva Visión.
Ciompi, L. (2007). Sentimientos, afectos y lógica afectiva: su lugar en nuestra comprensión del otro y del mundo. Revista de la Asociación Española de Neuropsiquiatría, 27(2), 153–71.
Clark, A. (1999). Estar ahí: cerebro, cuerpo y mundo en la nueva ciencia cognitiva. Barcelona: Paidós.
Csibra y Gergely, G. (2009). Natural pedagogy. Trends in cognitive sciences, 3(4), 148–53.
de La Bellacasa, M. P. (2017). Matters of care: Speculative ethics in more than human worlds. Minneapolis, MN: University of Minnesota Press.
De Waal, F. (2011). La edad de la empatía, ¿somos altruistas por naturaleza? Mexico: Tusquets.
Deleuze, G. (1973). Dualismo, monismo y multiplicidades [Course of March 26, 1973]. https://www.webdeleuze.com/textes/224
Deleuze, G. (1978). Sur Spinoza [Course of January 24, 1978]. https://www.webdeleuze.com/textes/12
Deleuze, G. (1980). Sur Spinoza [Course of November 25, 1980]. https://www.webdeleuze.com/textes/18
Deleuze, G. (1985). The intercessors [Interview with Antoine Dulaure and Claire Parnet]. L'Autre Journal, (8). http://lesilencequiparle.unblog.fr/2010/02/23/les-intercesseurs-gilles-deleuze/
Deleuze, G. y Guattari, F. (2004). Mil mesetas. Capitalismo y esquizofrenia. Valencia: Pre-Textos.

Descola, P. y P lsson, G. (Eds.) (2001). Naturaleza y cultura. Perspectivas antropológicas. Mexico: Siglo XXI.

Escobar, A. (2013). En el trasfondo de nuestra cultura: la tradición racionalista y el problema del dualismo ontológico. Tabula Rasa, (18), 15–42.

Escobar, A. (2016). Autonomía y diseño: la realización de lo comunal. Popayán, Colombia: Universidad del Cauca.

ETC Group. (2009). Who will feed us? Questions for the food and climate crisis. ETC Group Communiqué (102), 1.

Fernández, R. y González, L. (2014). En la espiral de la energía. Tomo II: Colapso del capitalismo global y civilizatorio. Madrid: Libros en Acción.

Fox, W. (1984). Deep ecology: A new philosophy of our time? The Ecologist, 14(5/6), 194–200.

Freeman, W. J. (1975). Mass action in the nervous system. Nueva York: Academic Press.

Fromm, E. (2000). El arte de amar. Buenos Aires: Paidós.

Gallagher, S. y Zahavi, D. (2014). La mente fenomenológica. Madrid: Alianza.

Geertz, C. (1991). La interpretación de las culturas. Barcelona: Gedisa.

Gibson-Graham, J. K. (1997). The end of capitalism (as we knew it): A feminist critique of political economy. Capital & Class, 21(2), 186–8.

Giraldo, O. F. (2014). Utopías en la era de la supervivencia. Una interpretación del buen vivir. México: Itaca.

Giraldo, O. F. (2018). Ecología política de la agricultura. Agroecología y posdesarrollo. San Cristóbal de Las Casas, Chiapas, México: Ecosur.

Giraldo, O. F. (2020). Cuerpos entre cuerpos, vida dentro de la vida, encuentros. Revista de Investigación Agraria y Ambiental, 11(3), 27–44.

Grosso, J. L. (2012). Del socioanálisis a la semiopraxis de la gestión social del conocimiento: contranarrativas en la telara a global. Popayán, Colombia: Universidad del Cauca.

Guattari, F. (1990). Las tres ecologías. Valencia, Espa a: Pre-Textos.

Hägerstrand, T. (1976). Geography and the study of the interaction between nature and society. Geoforum, 7(5–6), 329–34.

Han, B. C. (2016). Topología de la violencia. Barcelona: Herder.

Haskell, D. G. (2012). En un metro de bosque, un año observando la naturaleza. Madrid: Turner.

Heidegger, M. (1994). Construir, habitar, pensar. In M. Heidegger, Conferencias y artículos. Barcelona: Ediciones del Serbal.

Heidegger, M. (1996). La época de la imagen del mundo. In M. Heidegger, Caminos del bosque. Madrid: Alianza.

Hekimian, G. A. (2015). Ética del deseo. PhD Thesis in Philosophy, Universidad Complutense de Madrid.

Held, R. y Hein, A. V. (1958). Adaptation of disarranged hand-eye coordination contingent upon re-afferent stimulation. Perceptual and Motor Skills, 8(3), 87-90.

Hillman, H. (1991). La curación de la sombra. In C. Zweig y J. Abrams (Eds.), Encuentro con la sombra (pp. 161-2). Barcelona: Kairós.

Hoffman, M. L. (1992). Empathy and moral development. London: Cambridge University Press.

Hoffman, M. L. (2008). Empathy and prosocial behavior. In M. Lewis, J. M. Haviland-Jones y L. F. Barrett (Eds.), Handbook of emotions (pp. 440-55). Nueva York: Guilford Press.

Illich, I. (1997). The wisdom of Leopold Kohr. Bulletin of Science, Technology & Society, 17(4), 157-65.

Ingold, T. (1990) Society, nature and the concept of technology. Archaeological Review from Cambridge, 9(1), 5-17.

Ingold, T. (2000). The perception of the environment. Essays on livelihood, dwelling and skill. London: Routledge.

Ingold, T. (2001). El forrajero óptimo y el hombre económico. In En P. Descola y G. P lsson (Eds.), Naturaleza y sociedad. Perspectivas antropológicas. Mexico: Siglo XXI.

Ingold, T. (2008). Tres en uno: Cómo disolver las distinciones entre mente, cuerpo y cultura. In T. Sánchez (Ed.), Tecnogónesis, La construcción técnica de las ecologías humanas. Madrid: Antropólogos Iberoamericanos en Red.

Ingold, T. (2012). Ambientes para la vida. Montevideo: Trilce.

Ingold, T. (2015). Líneas: una breve historia. Barcelona: Gedisa.

Jarvis, E. D. (2004). Learned birdsong and the neurobiology of human language. Annals of the New York Academy of Sciences, 1016(1), 749-77.

Jha, A. (2015). The water book. Londres: Hachette.
Johnston, A. (2010). Fantasmas del pasado de las sustancias: Schelling, Lacan y la desnaturalización de la naturaleza. In En S. Žižek (Ed.), Lacan. Los interlocutores mudos (pp. 47–75). Madrid: Akal.
Jung, C. G. (2002). Arquetipos e inconsciente colectivo. Madrid: Trotta.
Kasperbauer, T. J. (2015). Rejecting empathy for animal ethics. Ethical Theory and Moral Practice, 18(4), 817–33.
Kusch, R. (1976). Geocultura del hombre americano. Buenos Aires: Fernando García Cambeiro.
Lacan, J. (2007). El Seminario 7. La ética del psicoanáisis. Buenos Aires: Paidós.
Land, E. H. (1977). The retinex theory of color vision. Scientific American, 237(6), 108–29.
Leff, E. (2002). Saber ambiental: sustentabilidad, racionalidad, complejidad, poder. Mexico: Siglo XXI.
Leff, E. (2004). Racionalidad ambiental. La reapropiación social de la naturaleza. Mexico: Siglo XXI.
Leff, E. (2014). La apuesta por la vida. Imaginación sociológica e imaginarios sociales en los territorios ambientales del sur. Mexico: Siglo XXI.
Leff, E. (2018). El fuego de la vida. Heidegger frente a la cuestión ambiental. Mexico: Siglo XXI.
Leff, E. (2021). El conflicto de la vida. Mexico: Siglo XXI Editores México.
León, E. (2011). El monstruo en el otro. Sensibilidad y coexistencia humana. Madrid: Sequitur.
León, E. (2017). Vivir queriendo: ensayos sobre las fuentes animadas de la afectividad. Madrid: Sequitur.
Levinas, E. (1987). De otro modo que ser o más allá de la esencia. Salamanca: Sígueme.
López-Intzín, J. (2015). Ich'el-ta-muk': la trama en la construcción del Lekilkuxlejal. Hacia una hermeneusis intercultural o visibilización de saberes desde la matricialidad del sentipensar-sentisaber tzeltal. In X. Leyva y A. K hler (Eds.), Prácticas otras de conocimiento(s). Entre crisis, entre guerras (Tomo I, pp. 181–98). Guadalajara: Casa del Mago.
Lovelock, J. (2007). La venganza de la tierra. Mexico: Planeta.

Macdonald, J. M. (1963). The threat to kill. American Journal of Psychiatry, 120(2), 125–30.

Madelin, P. (2016). Après le capitalisme: Essai d'écologie politique. Montreal: Ecosociété.

Madelin, P. (2020). Faut-il en finir avec la civilisation? Primitivisme et effondrement. Montreal: Ecosociété.

Mandoki, K. (2013). El indispensable exceso de la estética. Mexico: Siglo XXI.

Maturana, H. y Varela, F. (2003). El árbol del conocimiento. Las bases biológicas del conocimiento humano. Buenos Aires: Lumen.

Meltzoff y Moore, M. K. (1977). Imitation of facial and manual gestures by human neonates. Science, 198(4312), 75–8.

Merleau-Ponty, M. (1957). Fenomenología de la percepción. Mexico: Fondo de Cultura Económica.

Merleau-Ponty, M. (1968). The visible and the invisible. Evanston: Northwestern University Press.

Mier y Terán, M., Giraldo, O. F., Aldasoro, M., Morales, H., Ferguson, B., Rosset, P., Khadse, M. y Campos, A. (2018). Bringing agroecology to scale: Key drivers and emblematic cases. Agroecology and Sustainable Food Systems, 42(6), 637–65.

Morin, E. (1971). El paradigma perdido, Ensayo de bioantropología. Barcelona: Kairós.

Morin, E. (1986). El Método. La naturaleza de la naturaleza. Madrid: Cátedra.

Myin, E. y O'Regan, J. K. (2002). Perceptual consciousness, access to modality and skill theories. Journal of Consciousness Studies, 9(1), 27–45.

Naess, A. (1980). Environmental ethics and Spinoza's ethics. Inquiry, 23(3), 293–311.

Naess, A. (2007). The selected works of Arne Naess. Cham: Springer.

Nāgārjuna. (2004). Fundamentos de la vía media [Traducción directa del sánscrito]. Madrid: Siruela.

Nhat Hanh, T. (1975). The miracle of mindfulness. Boston: Beacon.

Noguera, A. P. (2004). El reencantamiento del mundo. Mexico: pnuma/Universidad Nacional de Colombia.

Noguera, A. P. (2012). Cuerpo-Tierra. El Enigma, El Habitar, La vida. Potencias de un Pensamiento Ambiental en clave del Reencantamiento del Mundo. Madrid: Editorial Académica Española.

Noguera, A. P. y Giraldo, O. F. (2017). ¿Para qué poetas en tiempos de extractivismo ambiental?. In H. Alimonda, C. Toro Pérez y F. Martín (Coords.), Ecología política latinoamericana. Pensamiento crítico, diferencia latinoamericana y rearticulación epistémica (pp. 69–93). Buenos Aires: Clacso.

Noguera, A. P., Ram rez, L. y Echeverry, S. (2020). Metodoestesis: los caminos del sentir en los saberes de la tierra. Una aventura geo-epistémica en clave sur. Revista de Investigación Agraria y Ambiental, 11(3), 45–64.

Oele, M. (2020). E-Co-Affectivity: Exploring Pathos at Life's Material Interfaces. New York: State University of New York Press.

Ospina, W. (2018). El taller, el templo y el hogar. Bogotá: Random House.

Oxley, J. (2011). The moral dimensions of empathy, limits and applications in ethical theory and practice. Nueva York: Palgrave Macmillan.

Pardo, J. L. (1991). Sobre los espacios pintar, escribir, pensar. Barcelona: Ediciones del Serbal.

Parkinson, C. (2019). Animals, anthropomorphism and mediated encounters. London: Routledge.

Patterson, C. (2002). Eternal Treblinka: Our treatment of animals and the Holocaust. Herndon: Lantern Books.

Peñaranda, M. L. P. (2010). Fenomenología de la corporeidad emotiva como condición de la alteridad. Investigaciones Fenomenológicas, (2), 141–68.

Pepperberg, I. (2011). La evolución del lenguaje desde una perspectiva aviar. In G. Gutiérrez y M. R. Papini (Eds.), Darwin y las ciencias del comportamiento (pp. 451–74). Bogotá: Universidad Nacional de Colombia.

Pfattheicher, S., Sassenrath, C. y Schindler, S. (2016). Feelings for the suffering of others and the environment: Compassion fosters proenvironmental tendencies. Environment and Behavior, 48(7), 929–45.

Pineda Muñoz, J. A. (2014). Geopoética de la guerra: he escuchado música en el estruendo del combate y he hallado paz donde las bombas escupían fuego. PhD Thesis in Social Sciences, Childhood and Youth, Universidad de Manizales, Colombia.

Plumwood, V. (2002). Feminism and the mastery of nature. London: Routledge.
Plumwood, V. (2005). Environmental culture: The ecological crisis of reason. London: Routledge.
Poerksen, U. (1995). Plastic words: The tyranny of a modular language. University Park: Penn State Press.
Rivera-Núñez, T., Fargher, L. y Nigh, R. (2020). Toward an historical agroecology: An academic approach in which time and space matter. Agroecology and Sustainable Food Systems, 44(8), 975–1011.
Rizzolatti, G. y Craighero, L. (2004). The mirror-neuron system. Annual Review of Neuroscience, 27, 169–92.
Robert, J. y Rahnema, M. (2015). La potencia de los pobres. San Cristóbal de Las Casas, Chiapas, Mexico: Cideci/Unitierra.
Rosset, P. M. y Altieri, M. A. (2017). Agroecology: Science and politics. Rugby: Practical Action Publishing.
Ruiz Albarrán, E. I. (2018). Pensar la naturaleza con Lacan: significante, sujeto escindido y objeto a. Tópicos del Seminario (39), 125–45.
Scheler, M. (2003). Gramática de los sentimientos: lo emocional como fundamento de la ética. Barcelona: Crítica.
Schumacher, E. F. (2011). Lo pequeño es hermoso. Madrid: Akal.
Schütz, A. y Luckmann, T. (2003). Las estructuras del mundo de la vida. Buenos Aires: Amorrortu.
Segato, R. L. (2018). Contra-pedagogías de la crueldad. Buenos Aires: Prometeo Libros.
Sevillano, V., Corraliza, J. A. y Lorenzo, E. (2017). Spanish version of the dispositional empathy with nature scale/versión española de la escala de empatía disposicional hacia la naturaleza. Revista de Psicología Social, 32(3), 624–58.
Shultz, W. (2002). Empathizing with nature: The effects of perspective taking on concern for environmental issues-statis. Journal of Social Issues, 56(3), 391–406.
Sloterdijk, P. (2003). Crítica de la razón cínica. Madrid: Siruela.
Smith, A. (1941). Teoría de los sentimientos morales. Mexico: Fondo de Cultura Económica.

Soto-Torres, G. (2020). Es posible una ética ambiental en la escisión ser humano/naturaleza? In En A. P. Noguera (Comp.), Polifonías geo-político-poéticas del habitar sur (pp. 84–108). Manizales: Universidad Nacional de Colombia.

Spinoza, B. (2011). Ética. Madrid: Alianza.

Suárez, A. F. (2008). La sevicia en las masacres de la guerra colombiana. Análisis Político, 21(63), 59–77.

Taibo, C. (2016). Colapso: capitalismo terminal, transición ecosocial, ecofascismo. Madrid: Catarata.

Tam, K. P. (2013). Dispositional empathy with nature. Journal of Environmental Psychology (35), 92–104.

Teramitsu, I., Kudo, L. C., London, S. E., Geschwind, D. H. y White, S. A. (2004). Parallel FoxP1 and FoxP2 expression in songbird and human brain predicts functional interaction. Journal of Neuroscience, 24(13), 3152-63.

Thompson, E. (2001). Empathy and consciousness. Journal of consciousness studies, 8(5–6), 1–32.

Thompson, E. (2005). Empathy and human experience. Science, religion, and the human experience (27), 261–87.

Thompson, E. (2010). Mind in life. Cambridge, MA: Harvard University Press.

Todorov, T. (1987). La conquista de América: el problema del otro. Mexico: Siglo XXI.

Toro, I. F. (2021). Afectos en línea de fuga: la potencia del espacio intersticial en San Cristóbal de Las Casas. Mexico: Cesmeca, Universidad de Ciencias y Artes de Chiapas.

Trías, E. (1991). Lógica del límite. Barcelona: Destino.

Turing, A. M. (1990). The chemical basis of morphogenesis. Bulletin of Mathematical Biology, 52(1–2), 153–97.

Uexküll, J. V. (1942). Meditaciones biológicas. Teoría de la significación. Madrid: Revista de Occidente.

Uribe, M. V. (2018). Antropología de la inhumanidad: Un ensayo interpretativo sobre el terror en Colombia. Bogotá: Universidad de los Andes.

Val, V., Rosset, P. M., Zamora, C., Giraldo, O. F. y Rochelau, D. (2019). Agroecology and La Vía Campesina I. The symbolic and material construction of agroecology through the dispositive of "peasant to peasant" processes. Agroecology and Sustainable Food Systems, 43(7–8), 872–94.

Valdés, F. (2018). Naxinandana chjota énná n´dexóa. Cerros aguas y pueblos: ecología política del territorio mazateco en San José Tengango, Oaxaca. Mexico: Bachelor's Thesis in Social Anthropology, Escuela Nacional de Antropología e Historia.

Van der Ploeg, J. D. (2013). Peasants and the art of farming: A Chayanovian manifesto. Rugby: Practical Action Publishing.

Varela, F., Thompson, E. y Rosch, E. (1997). De cuerpo presente. Las ciencias cognitivas y la experiencia humana. Barcelona: Gedisa.

Varela, F. (1992). La habilidad ética. Barcelona: Debate.

Varela, F. (2000). El fenómeno de la vida. Santiago de Chile: Dolmen Ediciones.

Varela, F. (2004). Monte grande [Video. Documentary film by F. Reichle, T. Zürich and C. Zürich]. https://www.youtube.com/watch?v=pf14LoBH37Q

Villafa a, A., Gil, S. y Gil, S. (2009). Palabras mayores [Documentary film by Centro de Comunicación Zhigoneshi, Organización Gonawind a Tayrona]. https://www.youtube.com/watch?v=rul8IzzebR8

Viveiros de Castro, E. V. (1998). Cosmological deixis and Amerindian perspectivism. Journal of the Royal Anthropological Institute, 4(3), 469–88.

Vreeke, G. J. y Van der Mark, I. L. (2003). Empathy, an integrative model. New Ideas in Psychology, 21(3), 177–207.

Wang, Y. M. (1963). Instructions for practical living and other neoconfucian writings. Princeton: University Press.

Weik von Mossner, A. (2017). Affective ecologies: Empathy, emotion, and environmental narrative. Ohio: The Ohio State University Press.

Žižek, S. (2001). El sublime objeto de la ideología. Mexico: Siglo XXI.

Žižek, S. (2005). La suspensión política de la ética. Mexico: Fondo de Cultura Económica.

Žižek, S. (2012). The pervert's guide to ideology. [Documentary film by Fienne, S. Zeitgeist Films].

Zweig, C. y Abrams, J. (1991). El lado oscuro de la vida cotidiana. In En C. Zweig y J. Abrams (Eds.), Encuentro con la sombra (pp. 7–13). Barcelona: Kairós.

Index

Abram, David 59, 60, 62, 70, 81, 111, 135
Aesthetic bios xiv 78, 79, 99, 130
Aesthetic compositions xii 77, 131
Affective economy 96, 97, 98, 100, 102, 114, 121
Affective environment 23, 59
Affective rails 97, 98, 101, 120, 131
Ángel Maya, Augusto 7, 8, 9, 11
Anthropocentric xiii, xiv, 28, 59, 103, 107, 110, 113, 120, 130

Bodies among bodies xi 1, 16, 31, 32, 37, 50, 53, 80, 121

Collapse viii 3, 33, 89, 90, 91, 92, 97, 119, 130

Deleuze, Gilles 5, 10, 11, 30, 31, 74, 143
Desire for life xiii, xiii, xiv 119, 126, 127, 128, 136
Dualisms xi 1, 2, 3, 5, 29, 35

Ecocidial shadow vi 113, 115, 116
Ecologies of cruelty xiii, xiv
Empathetic injustice 126, 129
Empathy vii, x, xi, xii, xiv 36, 43, 44, 45, 46, 47, 48, 49, 50, 51, 53, 54, 55, 56, 57, 58, 73, 77, 84, 85, 94, 95, 105, 106, 107, 113, 121, 130, 134
Enactive v 35, 37, 41, 45, 63
Encounters xvii 1, 13, 15, 16, 17, 18, 20, 21, 22, 24, 25, 26, 29, 30, 32, 37, 41, 42, 43, 45, 59, 62, 72, 77, 83, 84, 92
Entanglement 2, 11, 12, 13, 20, 30

Environmental affectivity ix, xiv, xv 12, 54, 62, 84, 92, 93, 95, 107, 121, 129, 130, 136, 137
Environmental crisis vii 2, 3, 4, 7, 9, 35
Environmental empathy xi, xii 36, 48, 52, 58, 77, 130, 134
Environmental epistemology x 1, 2
Environmental ethics ix, x, xi, xii, xiii, xiv, xv, xvi 1, 4, 29, 35, 36, 43, 52, 64, 65, 86, 89, 90, 91, 114, 116, 123, 125, 128, 135, 142
Environmental ethos 28, 29, 31, 88, 122, 125
Environmental knowledge xii, xiii, xiv, xvii 37, 62, 65, 66, 67, 69, 70, 74, 76, 79, 81, 82, 84, 85, 86, 92, 108, 109, 110, 112, 123, 125, 129, 130, 135, 136
Environmental thought vi, ix 1, 2, 3, 8, 13, 37, 41
Epistemo-aesthesis x, xi 8, 19, 28, 29, 31, 33, 136
Escobar, Arturo 3, 74, 146

Gallagher, Shaun 38, 40, 41, 46, 47, 50

Heidegger, Martin 3, 18, 19, 70

Ingold, Tim 11, 12, 13, 15, 17, 18, 56, 69, 76
Inhabiting-knowing 64, 83, 88
Insensitive x 106, 112, 113
Inter-being 16, 32, 137

Jung, Carl 113, 114

Index

Lacan, Jacques 6, 7, 9, 127, 148, 151
Language of the earth xii, xiv 59, 60, 62, 108, 110, 111, 113, 131
Latin American environmental thought ix, x 13
Leff, Enrique 3, 6, 7, 8, 9, 63, 123
León, Emma vi 15, 26, 64, 64, 95, 97
Levinas, Emmanuel 42, 43
Lines 11, 12, 13, 17, 73

Mandoki, Katya 13, 20, 22, 32, 61, 78, 79, 132
Merleu-Ponty, Maurice 38, 57, 59
Metaphysical 2, 7, 9, 10
Monisms x 1, 2, 29
Multiplicities xi 1, 10, 11, 18, 21, 23, 28, 29, 32, 36, 41, 56, 77, 85, 89, 95, 121

Neurophenomenology 37, 38, 42
Noguera, Patricia x, xv 13, 29, 31, 35

Ontological dualism 5, 9, 10
Ontological monism 5, 6, 7, 9, 10
Ordo amoris 97, 98, 101, 120, 131

Phenomenology vii, xii, xvii 30, 38, 43, 57, 60, 74, 75, 76, 111
Plastic words 109, 111, 120, 151

Plumwood, Val 3, 5, 6, 7, 8, 19
Proportionality 75, 76, 80, 81, 87, 88, 89, 91, 136

Regime of affectivity xiii, xiv 98, 99, 100, 101, 104, 106, 108, 111, 113, 114, 117, 120, 121, 122, 128, 129

Schütz, Alfred 66, 67, 68, 70
Sensory experience 42, 102, 136
Spinoza, Baruch ix, xvi 4, 6, 7, 8, 13, 16, 31, 57, 107, 125, 130
Sufficiency xiii 80, 81, 88

Thompson, Evan 14, 27, 37, 39, 40, 44, 45

Umwelt 23, 40, 58, 61, 98, 145

Varela, Francisco 13, 14, 19, 24, 26, 27, 29, 32, 37, 39, 40, 47, 54, 86
Vernacular knowledge xii 65, 66, 72, 73, 74, 75, 76, 78, 80, 93, 86

Web of life 5, 13, 22, 25, 87
Wisdom of the place 78, 79

Žižek, Slavoj 115, 123, 12

www.ingramcontent.com/pod-product-compliance
Lightning Source LLC
Chambersburg PA
CBHW070942040526
R18240200001BA/R182402PG44116CBX00017BA/5